AMERICAN
HERITAGE

October 1967 · Volume XVIII, Number 6

Essay: Filial Piety and the First Amendment

As much as it depends on its paper and ink, this magazine, like all books and periodicals published in this country, owes its continuing existence to the First Amendment to the Constitution of the United States, which guarantees freedom of speech and the press, and to the Fourteenth, which requires the states to respect the same rights. Whenever a threat to these liberties arises, therefore, we must resist it. For this reason AMERICAN HERITAGE and its editor have become involved, together with a great many eminent historians, in one of the most curious legal cases in recent years, that of *Frick v. Stevens.*

The facts are a little complicated. The elderly plaintiff, Miss Helen Clay Frick, the only surviving child of Henry Clay Frick, the noted Pittsburgh steel master who died in 1919, nearly a half century ago, is angry about a book which in a few cursory references makes what she regards as defamatory remarks about her father. She wants either to alter it or to win an injunction halting further distribution. The defendant is Dr. Sylvester K. Stevens, a professional historian, executive director of the Pennsylvania Historical and Museum Commission; he is also a member of the editorial Advisory Board of AMERICAN HERITAGE. His book, *Pennsylvania: Birthplace of a Nation,* was published by Random House in 1964. Miss Frick received a copy as a Christmas present and apparently turned at once to the index for references to her father.

What she found displeased her enormously, especially these two passages:

"In the bituminous coal fields of western Pennsylvania Henry Clay Frick had built a similar monopoly of coal and coke production and was equally successful in beating down efforts at unionization. Frick also made extensive use of immigrant labor and cut wages to an average of about $1.60 a day while extracting the longest hours of work physically possible. Most mines of the time were without anything resembling modern safety appliances or practices, and serious accidents were common.

"Still another abuse was the company town with its company store. The coal companies owned the houses, shoddy wooden shacks without sanitary facilities, which they rented at a high rate to workers."

. . .

"The power of the union was broken in the bloody and disastrous Homestead strike in 1892 by stern, brusque, autocratic Henry Clay Frick."

It does seem preposterous at this point in history and scholarship to protest such a mild view of a well-known figure in the harsh era of Rockefeller, Morgan, Fisk, Gould, and Carnegie. Hear, for example, what other historians have said about him:

"At the Homestead steel mills, Henry Frick displayed capitalist management in its ugliest and most relentless light . . ."

—Margaret Leech,
In the Days of McKinley

"Frick was instrumental in establishing the anti-union policy of the Carnegie partners. In 1890 he annihilated the union in the coke fields and in 1892 with Carnegie's approval directed the anti-union policy which brought on open warfare at Homestead. This strike started on July 1, 1892. Six days later 300 imported Pinkerton detectives, brought up the Ohio on barges, clashed with the unionists. After a bloody battle the detectives were escorted from town. On July 23, Alexander Berkman, an anarchist, attempted unsuccessfully to assassinate Frick. By fall hunger, dissension, and the repressive action of about 8,000 Pennsylvania guardsmen had broken the strike."

—*Encyclopedia of the Social Sciences*

"Frick was the personification of the ruthless business leader who would tolerate no opposition. His attitude toward labor was uncompromising."

—Philip Taft,
Organized Labor in American History

"One of the most notorious of all labor strikes was that at Homestead, Pennsylvania, in 1892. Beginning in a dispute over wages, it became a com-plicated case of the rights of private property against militant organized employees, a majority of whom were foreigners. Carnegie was in Scotland, and Frick was in full charge."

—*Dictionary of American Biography*

Why didn't Miss Frick sue some of these sources? Why didn't she, for that matter, sue such noted historians as Allan Nevins, Henry Steele Commager, and Samuel Eliot Morison, all of whom have had strong things to say of Henry Clay Frick? It turned out, in the Court of Common Pleas in Cumberland County, Pennsylvania, where she brought her suit, that Miss Frick had not read any such books. The kind of book she liked was *The Romance of Steel,* published in New York in 1907 and written by Herbert N. Casson. In this "very precious book," as Miss Frick called it, appeared a very different Frick:

". . . to the possession of this rare physical courage he adds the tenderest sentiment. His devotion to flowers, to painting and, above all, to his two children, Childs and Helen, is well known in Pittsburgh. . . . Mr. Frick has had a special checkbook made, which he uses for all charitable purposes; and upon every check is a picture of his daughter's face."

In her own complaint to the court, Miss Frick contemplates a figure scarcely recognizable to historians:

". . . an upright and honorable man, conducting all of his affairs in full compliance with all laws and with the highest principles of ethics and good conscience. . . . He treated working men fairly, paid wages which were reasonable and in line with the current conditions and raised them whenever possible, provided safety equipment of the best quality then in existence, and greatly improved the quality of homes rented to employees. . . ."

Although she is not personally mentioned in Dr. Stevens' book, Miss Frick believes that anything that historically blackens her father's character injures her reputation.

Henry Clay Frick was, in fact, a pretty tough old bird. Born of Mennonite and other German stock in 1849, and named for the great Whig compromiser, he went to work early for his grandfather, Abraham Overholt, a distiller of Youghiogheny whiskey whose name and countenance still adorn the label of a popular brand of oh-be-joyful. Serious, businesslike, hardworking, a character out of Horatio Alger, Frick moved on into coke and then steel, accumulated millions in his own right, and became a partner of and manager for Andrew Carnegie. Later in life he quarrelled with Carnegie, who was as hypocritical as Frick was straightforward about his wealth. In 1913, while breaking into New York society, Frick built a five-million-dollar house on Fifth Avenue at Seventy-First Street which, he said, would "make Carnegie's place look like a miner's shack." This truly handsome building he filled with paintings by El Greco, Van Dyck, Vermeer, Rembrandt, and Rubens, among others; on his death, when modern tax laws had begun to make their appearance, he left the home and its art to the public as The Frick Collection.

His loyal daughter was a strong character, too. She never married, and she devoted her career to continuing and augmenting her father's philanthropies, a Lady Bountiful with a whim of iron. According to a 1939 *New Yorker* article by John McCarten, she in those days hated wearers of bobbed hair, New Dealers, and (despite her antecedents) Germans. Out of her genuine love and knowledge of art, she built and organized, next door to her father's museum, the great Frick Art Reference Library, a superb scholarly institution that is a more durable achievement in its way than anything her father constructed. Generous and petty both, she for a long time excluded from it anyone with a German name until she decided that some of them might be just Americans who liked art, or that they could be Jews and other anti-Nazi refugees who had more reason than she for disliking Germany. (She was still angry from

The close relationship of Henry Clay Frick and his daughter Helen is symbolized in this double portrait by Edmund C. Tarbell. After her father died in 1919, Miss Frick kept the old family house in Pittsburgh, although she rarely lived there. She kept driving about in their old 1914 Pierce-Arrow and even maintained, unused, the Frick private railroad car.

the *First* World War.) She gave the public a nature sanctuary near her home in Westchester County, north of New York City, but threatened not long ago to repossess it if the Bureau of Public Roads went ahead with a plan to drive one of its big highways through it. Recently she has had a bitter controversy with the University of Pittsburgh, to which she has donated millions for an art building where she placed a collection of old masters. When Pitt incurred her displeasure by showing modern art and, in her opinion, otherwise misusing the building, she withdrew her financial support and her art. Lady Bountiful is apt to tie strings to her gifts.

There is an anachronistic air to the Fricks, father and daughter, that belongs to the era of great estates, large fortunes, forelock-tugging staffs, private railroad cars, and a kind of charitable disdain for the great unwashed. Mr. Frick abhorred publicity and avoided it all his life. Once, when the stock market was sinking and Mr. Frick was known to be conferring with James Stillman of the National City Bank, a financial writer whom both men respected found out about the meeting and sent in to seek their opinion. Out came, after an hour, this statement:

"The U.S.A. is a great and growing country.
　　　　　[signed] James Stillman
　　　　　　　　　 Henry C. Frick
This statement is confidential and not for publication unless names are omitted."

Miss Frick seems to dislike equally the glare of public attention, even when it is favorable. Many years ago she founded a retreat, or vacation home, for working girls at Beverly Farms, Massachusetts, not far from the family summer place at Prides Crossing. The retreat was later turned over to the Girls Clubs of America. In 1964, Mrs. Ellen Boyd, then a lady of eighty-six, who had worked at the home for some thirty years, privately printed an autobiography dealing largely with the history of this particular charity. Its references to Miss Frick were only devoted and laudatory, but the object of this gratitude was so distressed that she brought a suit in a

Massachusetts lower court to enjoin distribution of the book and have all copies suppressed. It is to the credit of the startled Massachusetts Supreme Judicial Court, where the matter was soon referred, that it threw out the case a month after the judges heard it, in January, 1966.

Unfortunately, no such thing happened in the suit against Dr. Stevens. The case was instituted in January, 1965, and dragged on until June, 1967, when Judge Clinton R. Weidner, in a most eloquent opinion, decided in favor of Dr. Stevens.

What then, since history has so far won out over filial piety, is the problem? In personal terms for Dr. Stevens, the case has been expensive in time and money; Miss Frick's financial resources are infinitely greater than his. In broader terms, the historical profession believes that this case ought to have been thrown out at the very start. It was not a libel suit, seeking damages, but one in equity, seeking a relief that is unconstitutional on its very face—an injunction against a book. The state judge considered the case both constitutionally and on its "merits," that is, on whether what Dr. Stevens wrote was accurate. He made it even more difficult by ruling out the testimony of professional historians who were waiting in court, and by excluding almost all "secondary" evidence (the writings of historians and other non-eyewitnesses). Only first-hand, contemporaneous evidence—either eyewitnesses or "disinterested" source materials—would do, went the ruling. No eyewitnesses, in fact, were introduced by either side in the trial, for the simple reason that they would have had to be about one hundred years old.

Deeply disturbed by the implications of this long-drawn-out suit, and by the preliminary rulings of the Pennsylvania court, a number of historians—representing the American Historical Association; the Organization of American Historians; our sponsors, the American Association for State and Local History and the Society of American Historians; and AMERICAN HERITAGE magazine—last year formed an *ad hoc* committee to fight this and any other infringement of the constitutional rights of historians to publish

freely. The editor of this magazine serves as treasurer. Money was raised to assist Dr. Stevens with his legal expenses and to bring a countersuit in the federal courts to enjoin Miss Frick from what we believe is her legal harrassment of Dr. Stevens.

An eminent former federal judge, Simon H. Rifkind, was retained as counsel in the countersuit. The very pendency of the Pennsylvania action, he contended, served to inhibit the rights of Dr. Stevens to publish freely, without malicious intent—even if what he had written was wrong. Judge Weidner, as it happens, has by painstaking effort satisfied himself that it was not wrong, but this is beside the point. The historians and Judge Rifkind claimed that a success for Miss Frick—indeed, even a long, costly delay—would inhibit the right of scholars "to speak freely about the past based on scholarly research, and . . . would permit the descendants of long-dead historical figures to have serious books removed from circulation simply because something critical was said about their ancestors."

As it turns out, the federal courts have been unwilling, on narrow grounds of jurisdiction, to relieve Dr. Stevens of his burden. The Supreme Court refused to hear the countersuit. However, since Miss Frick has appealed Judge Weidner's decision and has announced her intention to fight the case all the way, if necessary, the Supreme Court justices may eventually find these distinguished adversaries in their laps again, many printing and legal bills later. If they hear the case and do not clearly affirm the historian's right to be free of the burden of defending such suits, the time may be ripe for the descendants of Aaron Burr, Benedict Arnold, perhaps even George III, to hie them to the courts to "correct" the record. After that, of course, there will be a golden era for the writers of "authorized" biography who will advise us, *in extenso*, about the bravery of Burr, the kindness to animals of poor, misunderstood Arnold (about whom we are perhaps being actionable on pages 6 and 16 following), and the love of King George for his children. And you can forget the First Amendment.—*Oliver Jensen*

AMERICAN HERITAGE

The Magazine of History

SENIOR EDITOR
Bruce Catton

EDITOR
Oliver Jensen

MANAGING EDITOR
Robert L. Reynolds

ART DIRECTOR
Murray Belsky

ART EDITOR
Joan Paterson Kerr

ARTICLES EDITOR
E. M. Halliday

ASSOCIATE EDITORS
Robert S. Gallagher   David G. Lowe
Barbara Klaw   Douglas Tunstell

CONTRIBUTING EDITOR
Mary Cable

COPY EDITOR
Brenda Niemand

EDITORIAL ASSISTANTS
Mary Dawn Earley   Rosemary L. Klein
Mary A. Hawkins   Joanne Shapiro

PUBLISHER
Darby Perry

ADVISORY BOARD
Allan Nevins, *Chairman*
Carl Carmer   Louis C. Jones
Gerald Carson   Alvin M. Josephy, Jr.
Marshall B. Davidson   Howard H. Peckham
John A. Garraty   Francis S. Ronalds
Eric F. Goldman   S. K. Stevens

AMERICAN HERITAGE is published every two months by American Heritage Publishing Co., Inc., 551 Fifth Avenue, New York, N.Y. 10017.

PRESIDENT
James Parton

CHAIRMAN, EDITORIAL COMMITTEE
Joseph J. Thorndike

EDITORIAL DIRECTOR, BOOK DIVISION
Richard M. Ketchum

SENIOR ART DIRECTOR
Irwin Glusker

Correspondence about subscriptions should be sent to: American Heritage Subscription Office, 383 West Center Street, Marion, Ohio 43302. Single copies: $4.25. Annual subscriptions: $16.50 in U.S. and Canada; $17.50 elsewhere. An annual Index of AMERICAN HERITAGE is published in February, priced at $1.00. AMERICAN HERITAGE will consider but assumes no responsibility for unsolicited materials. Title registered U.S. Patent Office. Second-class postage paid at New York, N.Y., and at additional mailing offices.

Sponsored by

American Association for State & Local History · Society of American Historians

CONTENTS *October, 1967 · Volume XVIII, Number 6*

ESSAY: FILIAL PIETY AND THE FIRST AMENDMENT
by Oliver Jensen   2

BENEDICT ARNOLD:
HOW THE TRAITOR WAS UNMASKED
by James Thomas Flexner   6
THE AFTERMATH OF TREASON *by Milton Lomask* . . .   16

FACES FROM THE PAST—XXII *by Richard M. Ketchum* . . .   18

WHEN THE COACHMAN WAS A MILLIONAIRE
by Frank Kintrea   20

THE MARIANAS TURKEY SHOOT *by Admiral J. J. Clark* . . .   26

AMERICAN HERITAGE BOOK SELECTION
O-KEE-PA *by George Catlin*   30

OAK BLUFFS *by David G. McCullough*   38

DEATH ON THE RANGE *by David G. Lowe*   48

PICTURES WORTH A SECOND LOOK   50

CANYONLANDS *by Robert L. Reynolds*   52

CASEY AT THE BAT *by Martin Gardner*   64

READING, WRITING, AND HISTORY *by Bruce Catton* . . .   80

THE LIFE AND DEATH OF A GREAT NEWSPAPER
by Fred C. Shapiro   97

COVER: He did *not* say "Go West, young man, go West"; but he was always ready to give advice on almost any subject to Americans from Abraham Lincoln on down (or up, depending on his mood of the moment). Horace Greeley was the founder and, for over thirty years, the editor of New York's *Tribune*, a great newspaper the last incarnation of which recently disappeared forever from a rapidly dwindling journalistic field. An article on Greeley and the history of the *Tribune* starts on page 97; our cover portrays the rambunctious editor in his prime, shortly after the Civil War. *Back Cover:* The tough little baseball players displayed to celebrate the annual climax of our Great American Game are from trade cards circulated about 1880. We first guessed a considerably later date for them, but then we noticed that the players are barehanded, which puts them almost certainly before 1883; and the pitcher is asking the man at bat whether he will have his pitches high or low—a delightful option enjoyed by the batter between 1870 and 1887. Both covers come from Culver Pictures.

Benedict Arnold: How the Traitor Was Unmasked

By JAMES THOMAS FLEXNER

The most famous, or infamous, traitor in American history was Major General Benedict Arnold—a brilliant officer, a whirlwind hero, a trusted military comrade of George Washington's. The culmination of his treachery was a plot to deliver up West Point, America's strongest and most important fortification, to the British. AMERICAN HERITAGE presents in this issue two segments of Benedict Arnold's complex story. "How the Traitor Was Unmasked," by James Thomas Flexner, is the exciting and moving account of General Washington's discovery of his friend's "villainous perfidy"—an excerpt from Mr. Flexner's book, George Washington in the American Revolution, to be published early in 1968 by Little, Brown and Company. In "The Aftermath of Treason," beginning on page 16, Milton Lomask tells the story of the Arnolds' subsequent life in England and Canada.   —The Editors

As he rode back toward his army after a frustrating conference with his French allies at Hartford, Connecticut, on September 24, 1780, George Washington felt the need of some gaiety to raise his melancholy spirits. He looked forward eagerly to a relaxed evening at the home of old friends—his military comrade Benedict Arnold and Arnold's pretty wife, Peggy, whom Washington had known since she was a girl. The Commander in Chief intended to enjoy his dinner and a good night's rest, and then to spend the next day inspecting the great patriot fortification at West Point, which Arnold now commanded.

Business, however, intervened. On the road he met the French ambassador, Chevalier Anne Cesar de la Luzerne, and had to pause for further involved negotiations. He spent the night at Fishkill, New York.

Early the next morning, as soon as the autumnal sky

If I point out a plan of coöperation by which S. H. shall possess himself of West Point, the Garrison, &c. &c. &c. twenty thousand pounds Sterling I think will be a cheap purchase for an object of so much importance. At the same time I request a thousand pounds to be paid my Agent—

This is the decoded British copy of Arnold's offer to deliver up West Point to Sir Henry Clinton ("S. H.") for twenty thousand pounds, a sum equivalent to a half million dollars today. The letter was sent two months before the events in our story.

began to lighten, Washington set out again on his interrupted journey. It was only a short ride to Arnold's headquarters, but there were redoubts along the river that Washington felt he ought to visit. As he repeatedly turned off the highroad down lanes rutted by the wheels of cannon, his companions—the Marquis de Lafayette, the artillery general Henry Knox, and a flock of aides—became impatient. Eventually, Lafayette (so it is reported) reminded Washington that Mrs. Arnold was waiting breakfast for them.

The Commander replied genially, "Ah, I know you young men are all in love with Mrs. Arnold. . . . You may go and take your breakfast with her, and tell her not to wait for me." Lafayette and most of the party decided to stay with his Excellency, but two aides, Captain Samuel Shaw and Major James McHenry, rode ahead with the message.

Inspection takes time, and the morning was far advanced before Washington finally glimpsed Arnold's headquarters through the trees. Robinson's House stood on the east bank of the Hudson, about a mile and a half below West Point. Correct eighteenth-century gentlemen considered that the location—"surrounded on two sides by hideous mountains and dreary forests, [and] not a house in view but one within a mile"—could appeal only to "a taste for romantic singularity and novelty." But Washington looked forward to a warm welcome: the firm handshake of Arnold, and the winning smiles of sweet, blonde, girlish Peggy.

He spurred his horse slightly and approached the rambling, capacious two-story mansion house. Since he had sent four light-horsemen to alert the Arnolds of his immediate arrival, he expected to find that friendly couple waiting at the door to greet him. He saw instead a foppish young man who stood alone,

bowing a meticulously powdered head, while embarrassment marked his features. Washington probably recognized Arnold's aide, David Salisbury Franks. In voluble sentences punctuated by nervous giggles, Franks stated that Mrs. Arnold had not yet arisen and that the General had left by water for West Point. The General had told Franks that he was on his way to prepare a suitable welcome for his Excellency. Had his Excellency breakfasted? When Washington said he had not, Franks bustled off to get food on the table.

This greeting was disappointing. But Washington knew that it was natural for belles to sleep late, and he could not have been displeased that Arnold was preparing a reception for him, since he believed that ceremonies of respect to high officers improved both the appearance and the discipline of an army. He ate a leisurely breakfast. Then, leaving his aide Colonel Alexander Hamilton behind to receive any dispatches, he descended with a small group to the landing where a barge and its oarsmen were waiting to transport him to West Point.

The oarsmen created ripples in the water as they rowed, and the fortress came ever more clearly into view. It seemed to slant backward as it mounted the precipitous west shore of the river. Not very far above the water, Fort Arnold, the main redoubt, clung to a sheer crag like a monstrous crab. As the surrounding hills billowed higher, they revealed ramparts pierced for cannon, while near the sky three peaks were topped with semi-independent forts. The mazelike, interweaving walls were built of a mixture of wood, turf, and stone. Scars on the hillsides spoke of quarrying too recent to have greened over, and piles of rocks and logs indicated construction still only planned. Washington knew that a short distance downstream the river washed from bank to bank over the links of a

7

On the way to Arnold's headquarters, Washington stopped frequently to inspect troops stationed along the Hudson.

tremendous iron chain resting on huge logs. On this spot the main cannon were trained.

Washington must have been moved as the fortress came closer. This was the great engineering feat of his command, the only truly strong point created by the Continental Army. Volunteer engineers from abroad had designed it. During more than three years of hard labor, soldiers had shaped the towering ramparts. Inflated dollars, raised with anguish, had been spent by the millions. And there the fortress stood, serene in the pellucid autumn air, while Benedict Arnold— so Washington believed—was preparing the garrison for a military greeting to the Commander in Chief.

As Washington's barge drew close to the beach and landing wharf these proved to be surprisingly empty— no bustle of officers lining up men; only the usual sentries somnolently pacing. Washington then saw Colonel John Lamb, the resident commandant of the fortress, come running down the steep road from the main redoubt. Still out of breath when Washington stepped ashore, Lamb puffed out apologies for having prepared no suitable reception. If only he had been notified!

To Washington's startled query, Lamb replied that he had not seen Arnold that day. This seemed strange

—but there were various landing places under the redoubts. Perhaps Arnold had come another way.

The inspection began. As Washington climbed over the hillsides, ducked through blockhouse doors, and visited gun emplacements, he asked everywhere for Arnold. "No one could give me any information where he was," the General wrote later. "The impropriety of his conduct, when he knew I was to be there, struck me very forcibly." Washington became increasingly anxious. "My mind misgave me, [but] I had not the least idea of the real cause."

Washington was later to insist that he had found the post in "a most critical condition." However, he probably was not particularly upset about this at the time. If some of the redoubts were weak, broken, or unfinished, if work seemed to be progressing slowly, he could hardly have been surprised. Perfection rarely hovered over the Continental Army.

Dinner at the Arnolds' had been set for four o'clock. Washington completed his inspection in time to permit his rowers to get him back to Robinson's House by three thirty. He strode anxiously up the steep bluff from the riverbank, but again the opening door revealed neither Arnold nor Peggy. It was Alexander Hamilton who greeted him. No, Hamilton had heard nothing of Arnold. No, Peggy had not emerged from her bedroom; she had sent down word that she was indisposed.

Washington walked along a hallway to the chamber that had been assigned to him and began to freshen up for the meal. There was a knock on the door. Hamilton came in carrying a handful of papers. Washington reached out for the packet and began to read.

In another room on the same floor Lafayette was washing up when Hamilton suddenly burst open the door. He begged the Marquis to attend instantly on his Excellency. Lafayette sprinted down the hall to find Washington trembling with emotion. "Arnold has betrayed us!" Washington cried out. "Whom can we trust now?"

The first task, as soon as the men had regained enough control to think rationally, was to determine by a careful examination of the many papers exactly what the situation was. There must have been (although it is now lost) a covering letter from the outpost commander, Lieutenant Colonel John Jameson, stating that three irregulars had been prowling in the British-dominated territory beyond the Croton River on Saturday, September 23, when they stopped a lone rider in civilian clothes. The rider, who stated that his name was John Anderson, behaved so strangely that they stripped him. They found documents in his shoes. Jameson was holding the man and was herewith forwarding the documents.

Right: Though this portrait of Peggy Arnold and one of her children was painted years later in London, it helps us to understand how the distraught, pretty young mother had so easily persuaded the chivalrous General Washington of her "innocence." Washington was always susceptible to feminine beauty. The artist was Daniel Gardner. Robinson's House, below, where Peggy's histrionics took place, was so called after its exiled Tory owner. Arnold used the building as both his residence and his military headquarters.

There was an official pass allowing "John Anderson" to move between the lines—made out by Benedict Arnold. Also in Arnold's handwriting were a transcript of secret information Washington had given a council of war, pages of material about West Point that would be useful to a besieger, and a rough accounting of the fort's 3,086 men, patriots whom Arnold had slated for death or capture.

A later addition to the packet was a letter, meticulously executed in an elegant script. It proved to be from the prisoner: "I beg your Excellency will be persuaded that no alteration in the temper of my mind, or apprehension for my safety, induces me to take the step of addressing you, but that it is to secure myself from an imputation of having assumed a mean character for treacherous purposes or self-interest, a

9

This nineteenth-century map depicts the scene of our story —Robinson's House and West Point near the top; Tarry-town, near which André was captured, at lower right; the narrows of the Hudson (middle of map), where H.M.S. Vulture hovered, waiting for Arnold; and Tappan (lower left), where André was hanged. The menacing dagger and the coiled snake clearly suggest that this is a Map of Treason.

conduct incompatible with the principles that actuate me, as well as with my condition in life. . . . The person in your possession is Major John André, Adjutant General to the British army."

For a general to try to capitalize on the wavering loyalty of an adversary, André continued, was a legitimate "advantage taken in war." To further such an end, "I agreed to meet, upon ground not within the posts of either army, a person who was to give me intelligence; I came up [the Hudson] in the *Vulture*, man of war, for this effect, and was fetched by a boat from the shore to the beach. Being there I was told that the approach of day would prevent my return, and that I must be concealed until the next night. I was in my regimentals and had fairly risked my person."

The rest of André's account was intended, as Washington later put it, "to show that he did not come under the description of a spy." He had been conducted against his will and without his knowledge, André wrote, behind the American lines. He had thus

been forced by circumstances beyond his control to remove his uniform and put on a civilian disguise. He had become, in effect, a prisoner of war. "I had to concert my escape. . . . I was taken at Tarry Town by some volunteers."

After Washington had read all the documents, the question was what to do. A glance out the window would have shown that the wind, blowing upriver, was ideal for carrying British ships from their anchorages in New York Harbor to the West Point Arnold clearly intended to betray. Washington could not know to what extent other officers were involved in the plot; he could not be sure that, even though André had been intercepted, duplicate documents had not got through to the British. However, overriding emotions kept Washington from deciding that his first duty was to take every step to protect the endangered fortress.

The most important consideration, so it seemed to Washington, was to capture and hang the traitor. Although McHenry, who had breakfasted with Arnold, reported that the villain had disappeared immediately after receiving a letter that had thrown him "into some degree of agitation," Washington refused to accept the conclusion that Arnold had been notified of André's capture and had surely made his escape during the intervening five hours. Perhaps he was lurking somewhere within the lines, still ignorant of his danger. Under these circumstances, Washington thought, no move should be made that would indicate to anyone who might alert Arnold that the treason had been discovered. While all else went on as usual, Hamilton and McHenry should gallop, as fast as the swiftest horses could carry them, to King's Ferry, eight miles downriver, where there were forts and forces that could stop Arnold's barge "if she had not passed."

No sooner had Hamilton and McHenry pounded off than Arnold's senior aide, Lieutenant Colonel Richard Varick, who had been in bed with a fever, came into Washington's room. He was flushed, a little unsteady, and clearly in the grip of strong emotion. He said that Mrs. Arnold seemed to have gone mad. She had run through the halls half dressed, and, after he had got her back in bed, she exclaimed that "there was a hot iron on her head, and no one but General Washington can take it off." Would his Excellency please go to the anguished lady?

Washington mounted the stairs to Peggy's room. In her disarranged bed, with her hair flying around her touching face and her nightclothes pulled awry, she exhibited, so Hamilton was told, "all the sweetness of beauty, all the loveliness of innocence, all the tenderness of a wife, and all the fondness of a mother. . . . One moment she raved, another she melted into tears. Sometimes she pressed her infant to her bosom." She dandled her babe wide-eyed and seemed oblivious of her visitors. Finally Varick said, "There is General Washington."

As Washington leaned over her, his features working with pity, she stared him hard in the face.

"No! That is not Washington!"

Gently, he tried to assure her.

"No!" she cried again, gesturing with her bare, shapely arms to shield her infant. "No, that is not General Washington; that is the man who was agoing to assist Colonel Varick in killing my child."

Washington labored to disabuse her, but when she finally admitted that he was indeed Washington, it was only to upbraid him for "being in a plot to murder her child." Her husband, she cried out, could not protect her: "General Arnold will never return; he is gone; he is gone forever; *there, there, there*: the spirits have carried [him] up there. . . ." She pointed at the ceiling. "They have put hot irons in his head."

As the lovely lady raved and gestured, her clothes sometimes parted to reveal charms that should have been hidden. Then she would push her baby aside and turn downward on the bed to cling to the mattress in a transport of tears. At last, finding that he could not make her respond to his reassurances, Washington sadly went away, probably hating Arnold all the more for having caused such anguish to a beauty he never doubted was innocent.

That Peggy had been in the plot from the start, and may even have instigated it, was, indeed, to remain a secret until the relevant British headquarters papers were made public in the 1930's. In any case, Washington always shied away from connecting the fair sex with the dark emotions of war. Peggy—who had been warned by Arnold before he fled that the treason had been discovered—need not have used such heavy emotional artillery to convince the courtly commander that she was a greatly wronged angel. He left her bedroom determined to protect her from every implication raised by her husband's guilt.

He went down the stairs and joined an uneasy group of officers in the living room. "Mrs. Arnold is sick," Washington said, "and General Arnold is away. We must therefore take our dinner without them."

"I had a high fever," Varick later wrote, "but officiated at the head of the table." Both he and Franks, who had taken no part in the plot, had by now inferred that Arnold had gone to the enemy. Unwilling to accuse their superior without real evidence, and realizing that if treason had taken place they would be under suspicion, they watched Washington covertly for indications of what he knew and how he felt toward them. Washington and his staff were at the same time surreptitiously watching them for signs of guilt.

"Never," Lafayette is quoted as reminiscing, "was there a more melancholy dinner. The General was silent and reserved, and none of us spoke of what we were thinking about. . . . Gloom and distress seemed to pervade every mind, and I have never seen General Washington so affected by any circumstance." However, Washington's courtesy did not desert him. Varick noted that "his Excellency behaved with his usual affability and politeness to me."

The food, "plentiful" but hardly touched, was finally cleared away. The parties separated. After a while, Washington asked Varick to put on his hat. As they walked outside, Washington told him of Arnold's perfidy. Then (so Varick wrote), "with delicacy, tenderness, and civility," Washington stated that, although "he had not the least cause of suspicion of Major Franks or myself," the two must consider themselves under arrest. "I then told him the little all I knew."

André had now been a captive for more than two days. It would have been a poor spy network indeed that was not pulsing out warnings, and any hope of gain to be achieved through secrecy would seem to be over. The wind was still blowing upriver. If Arnold had placed at key positions officers who were his partners in the plot, they still held their commands. West Point had not been alerted. Yet Washington still took no active steps. The man who had admired and trusted Arnold, and to whom treason was personally inconceivable, was circling in the murky mazes of what Varick called "the most affecting and pungent anxiety and distress."

Between six and seven that evening, Washington received a letter from Hamilton at King's Ferry stating that Arnold had escaped to the *Vulture*, the British warship that had brought André and then anchored in the river. "I do not believe the project will go on," Hamilton continued, "yet it is possible Arnold has made such dispositions with the garrison as may tempt the enemy, in its present weakness, to make the stroke tonight.". . . "Without making a bustle," Hamilton was notifying the commander of the main army in New Jersey, General Nathanael Greene, "to be in readiness to march and even to detach a brigade this way." He hoped Washington would approve, "as there may be no time to lose."

Hamilton enclosed two letters that had been sent from the *Vulture* to King's Ferry. Both were in Arnold's familiar handwriting. The one addressed to Washington contended defiantly that, whatever the misguided might think, it was true patriotism that had carried Arnold to the British. The second letter was addressed to Peggy. Washington sent it upstairs unopened, accompanied by a message saying that, although it was his duty to try to capture Arnold, he was happy to relieve her anxiety by telling her that her husband was safe.

Washington could hardly have helped recognizing that he had been derelict in not ordering Hamilton to do what the aide had done on his own: warn the commander of the main army to be prepared. This realization, plus the news that Arnold had actually escaped, seems to have shaken him out of his lethargy. In a series of hasty dispatches he changed the commanders at outposts where Arnold might have placed collaborators; and he alerted West Point, ordering that it be reinforced and put in readiness for an attack.

Washington's long and dangerous delay in acting to protect West Point is sometimes overlooked in history books as a matter that does not contribute to the conventional image of the General's unshakable perfection. The author of his most massive biography, Douglas Southall Freeman, who did recognize the facts, tried to explain them away by stating that not until evening did Washington know "enough about the situation" to take action. However, many of the orders Washington finally gave did not depend on specific information, and, in any case, Colonel Lamb, the officer most familiar with the situation at West Point, had returned with Washington from the fort to Robinson's House and was available for consultation. The truth seems to be that Washington's mind was thrown into such a turmoil that he was for a time immobilized, incapable of clear thought.

Luckily, no harm resulted. During the night the wind changed; blowing downriver, it erased the possibility that the British could gain any direct military advantage from Arnold's treason. They had not, indeed, planned any immediate action. Nor did they even know that Arnold and André had actually concerted a plan until, to their amazement, Arnold appeared alongside the *Vulture* and reported André's capture, which had given everything away.

As the possibility of a successful British attack evaporated, the immediate tension at Robinson's House eased. However, Washington still had to handle his own emotions; to question whether there were more traitors to be discovered; and to face the frightening problem of how the treason of so conspicuous an officer could be prevented from psychologically damaging the already flagging Revolutionary cause.

The human problem closest to Washington's emotions was twenty-year-old Peggy, "whose face and youthfulness [as Lafayette wrote] make her so interesting." In the morning she admitted to no memory of her hysteria of the day before, and now spoke frankly, if tearfully, of her apprehension that "the resentment of her country will fall upon her who is only unfortunate." Washington was all sympathy and grave reassurance; he offered to send her either to her husband in New York or to her father in Philadelphia. She chose to turn her back on the plot that had failed; Franks accompanied her to Philadelphia. "It would be extremely painful to General Washington," Lafayette wrote to Luzerne, "if she were not treated with the greatest kindness."

By Washington's order, the various individuals known to have been concerned in André's foray into American-held territory were now gathered at Robinson's House. Interviewing them himself, Washington decided that only one man was sufficiently implicated to be tried. He was the local landowner, Joshua Hett Smith, who had served as André's companion behind the American lines. In the end, Smith was demonstrated to have been a fool rather than a villain. He had simply believed what Arnold had told him: that André was not a British but an American spy, whom it was his patriotic duty to help. Court-martialled at their own request so that their names could be cleared, Varick and Franks were proved completely innocent. Arnold, it was concluded, had operated as a lone wolf.

After André had been brought to headquarters, Washington found him "a man of the first abilities" and treated him, so the Briton wrote Clinton, "with the greatest attention." André was, indeed, a prisoner to wring Washington's heart. Of French background,

Arnold's Plot: In these highly romanticized nineteenth-century views, Arnold, at left, plots darkly in the woods with André; at center, he tells André to conceal the military secrets in his boot; at right, Peggy swoons when Arnold says he must flee.

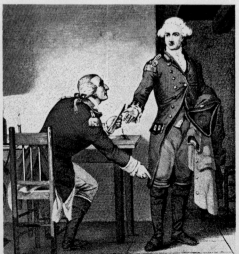

although born in London, he had marked temperamental resemblances to Washington's beloved Lafayette; he was also young enough to be Washington's son. He was quick, mercurial, brilliant, chivalrous, and much concerned with personal honor. In a situation of mortal danger, he displayed—could Lafayette have done it as well?—almost superhuman control. He behaved in the presence of his captors with charm, grace, almost relaxation.

To Washington, as to all the other officers concerned, André's plight was particularly poignant because the young man's own romantic impetuosity had placed him in a predicament that the eighteenth century considered far below his station. Gentlemen could be spy masters, but they did not themselves wear disguises and rummage behind enemy lines. André continued to claim that he had come ashore in his regular uniform in a high official capacity, and had been tricked by Arnold into entering an American post. Once there, so his argument went, he could not possibly have escaped as long as he was wearing the British uniform. To the captors, hatred for Arnold made this believable, yet the fact remained that André had been caught in civilian clothes, bearing incriminating papers, and functioning as a spy. The established punishment for that was not a gentleman's death—being shot—but the death of a varlet—being dangled from a gallows.

The meanness of his situation spurred André into a high line of "candor." To the board of general officers who conducted his trial, he confessed so much that the verdict was inevitable. The board ruled that he "ought to be considered as a spy from the Enemy, and that agreable to the Law and usage of Nations it is their opinion he ought to suffer death."

From André, Washington received a letter that the condemned man signed with his proud title, Adjutant General to the British Army:

Buoyed above the terror of death by the consciousness of a life devoted to honourable pursuits, and stained with no action that can give me remorse, I trust that the request I make to your Excellency at this serious period, and which is to soften my last moments, will not be rejected.

Sympathy toward a soldier will surely induce your Excellency and a military tribunal to adopt the mode of my death to the feelings of a man of honour.

Let me hope, Sir, that if aught in my character impresses you with esteem towards me, if aught in my misfortunes marks me as the victim of policy and not of resentment, I shall experience the operation of these feelings in your breast, by being informed that I am not to die on a gibbet.

The consideration was one that Washington, as a gentleman, could not help but find affecting—and he was always unhappy about executions. To make matters worse, his brilliant young officers were almost swooning with admiration and pity for André. Hamilton, to whom the prisoner had made a personal appeal, was particularly insistent, even rude, and went off in a rage when Washington would not agree that André be shot. "Some people," Hamilton growled, "are only sensible to motives of policy!" Yet Washington felt he had no choice. British propaganda was shouting that André's arrest had been an atrocity. If he were not executed in the manner of a spy it would be considered proof that he had not really been a spy but had been wantonly murdered.

André occupied the same position in Clinton's heart that Lafayette did in Washington's. Across the lines came letters in which Clinton insisted that his friend had gone on an official mission to Arnold, and had subsequently merely obeyed orders that Arnold, as commander in the area, had a right to give. This argument was specious (a spy is not blameless because he obeys the orders of the traitor he is suborning), and it also contradicted André's own contention that Arnold had carried him behind the American lines without his knowledge and against his will. However, Washington saw in Clinton's concern a chance of saving the young man whom he considered "more unfortunate than criminal" and who had "much in his character to interest."

Arnold's Escape: At left, British boatmen wait to whisk the traitor away; at center, they row out to the waiting Vulture; *at right, the villain, looking dejected (probably disappointment rather than a bad conscience), boards the British ship.*

The three irregulars who captured André were probably looking for British soldiers or Tories; a local law allowed them to claim property found on a captured enemy. André was dressed in civilian clothes, but his evasive answers led the irregulars to search him, and the incriminating papers were found in his boot. This painting ennobles the motives of the captors.

Washington might "lament," but he recognized a "necessity of rigor": the Army was in effect on trial in the eyes of the American people. To spare the British agent outright would be interpreted as softness about treason. But supposing Washington could substitute on the gallows the real, the heinous criminal?

Captain Aaron Ogden of the light infantry had been ordered to appear at headquarters, now at Tappan, New York, at the dot of eight o'clock on the morning after André was sentenced. To his surprise, he found his Excellency waiting for him outside the door. Washington handed him some letters to take under a flag of truce to the British lines, and then told him to go to Lafayette's tent for further instructions. Lafayette was also eagerly awaiting him. Suggesting

what Washington could not personally, Lafayette urged Ogden to whisper to the British commander "that if Sir Henry Clinton would ... suffer General Washington to get within his power General Arnold, then Major André should be immediately released."

Ogden did as he was told, and the British officer who had met his flag leaped on a horse and galloped away. In two hours he was back with a glum face and the verbal answer: "A deserter was never given up." He also brought written information that a high-level British delegation would come to the American lines to intercede for André.

The resulting meeting was useless. The British representatives had nothing more to present than the arguments that had already been submitted to Washington in writing. Deeply disappointed, Washington set the execution for noon the next day, October 2.

The macabre procession from André's place of confinement to the gallows would pass close to Washington's headquarters; the death march would pound in, even through closed windows. To allow the sufferer hope, Washington had not notified him of how he was to be executed, and there would be the dreadful moment when the young British gentleman saw the gallows. It was not an agreeable moment to contemplate.

When the execution was over, Washington was surrounded by men in tears. They recounted how André had himself bared his neck for the hangman and had drawn the knot close under his right ear. His last words had been, "I have nothing more to say, gentlemen, than this. You will all bear witness that I have met my fate as a brave man."

In Washington's headquarters, eyes were still wet when a belated dispatch appeared from the British lines. It was a letter from Benedict Arnold threatening that if André were executed, he personally would "think myself bound by every tie of duty and honour to retaliate on such unhappy persons of your army as may fall within my power.... I call Heaven and earth to witness that your Excellency will be justly answerable for the torrent of blood that may be spilt in consequence!"

"There are no terms," Washington wrote of Arnold, "that can describe the baseness of his heart." Shortly afterward he instigated an elaborate plot (which misfired) to kidnap the traitor from his lodgings in New York City and bring him out alive for hanging to patriot cheers (see "The Sergeant Major's Strange Mission" in the October, 1957, AMERICAN HERITAGE).

As British propagandists ground out statements attributed to Arnold in which he described his treason as true patriotism and urged his former associates to imitate him, hatred for the traitor swept the nation. Washington, who was not without enemies, had in the past consistently supported Arnold to the civilian authorities; he had personally placed him in command at West Point. And the whole conservative wing of the Revolutionary leadership was liable to the charge of guilt by association, since they had backed Arnold when he had been attacked by the radicals who controlled the government of Pennsylvania. As the leader of those radicals, Joseph Reed did make gestures at demonstrating that Washington had shown gross favoritism to the traitor, but even Reed was half-hearted—glad, it seemed, quickly to abandon his efforts. In the end, the Pennsylvania radicals contented themselves with banishing Peggy from her father's house in Philadelphia. She was forced to join her partner in treason behind the British lines.

One trembles to think what a modern "superpatriot" rabble-rouser might have done with the issue. However, our forefathers resisted all temptation to shatter the precarious national unity. Washington's own attitude was expressed in dismissing a rumor that another American general, Robert Howe, was in the pay of the British. He wrote the Board of War that they ought not to "neglect any clues that may lead to discoveries, but, on the other hand, we ought to be equally circumspect in admitting suspicions or proceeding upon them without sufficient evidence. It will be the policy of the enemy to distract us as much as possible by sowing jealousies . . ."

Washington labored to turn the popular emotion against Arnold to gratitude that the plot had been foiled. "In no instance since the commencement of the war," he stated, "has the interposition of Providence appeared more conspicuous than in the rescue of the post and garrison of West Point from Arnold's villainous perfidy."

The hanging of Major André, and his nobility in the face of death, moved witnesses to tears. "The Unfortunate Death of Major André" illustrated a British history book.

SACRED to the MEMORY
of
MAJOR JOHN ANDRE
who was raised by his Merit at an early period of Life to the rank of Adjutant General
of the British Forces in America
and employ'd in an important but hazardous Enterprise
fell a Sacrifice to his Zeal for his KING and COUNTRY
on the 2 of OCTOBER A.D. 1780
Aged 29
universally Beloved and esteem'd by the Army in which he Served
and lamented even by his
FOES
His Gracious Sovereign KING GEORGE the THIRD
has caused this Monument
to be erected

Benedict Arnold: *The Aftermath of Treason*

By MILTON LOMASK

One day in the winter of 1782–83, an exiled American neutralist, Peter Van Schaack by name, was browsing through London's Westminster Abbey when he was startled to see a familiar figure standing before a newly erected monument to Major John André, the young British officer who had collaborated with Benedict Arnold in the unsuccessful scheme to betray West Point. The thickset, hulking-shouldered man who was reading the tribute to the fallen soldier's "Zeal for his KING and COUNTRY" on the marble face of the cenotaph was Benedict Arnold himself.

"What a spectacle!" Van Schaack's son and biographer wrote later. "The traitor Arnold, in Westminster Abbey, at the tomb of André, deliberately perusing the monumental inscription, which will transmit to future ages the tale of his own infamy!"

Arnold was not alone. At his side was a young

Two years after André's execution, a hero's monument (opposite) was raised in his honor in Westminster Abbey. Meanwhile, Americans had commemorated Arnold's role in the affair with a parade (below) in Philadelphia featuring a two-faced effigy of the traitor, on his way to hell-fire under the auspices of his master, a ferocious-looking devil.

woman. Van Schaack had never met the former Margaret Shippen, the golden-haired Philadelphia aristocrat who a few years before had become the second Mrs. Benedict Arnold; but her appealing features had been described to him. He recognized her at once, and even as he turned from the scene "in disgust," he must have found himself wondering what it was like to be the wife of the most despised man of his generation. What did life hold, after treason, for the exiled Benedict Arnolds?

Biographers have found partial answers in many scattered sources—in the London press, for example, which occasionally mentioned the Arnolds; or in the voluminous correspondence Peggy Arnold carried on with her family and friends in America. The picture that emerges is bittersweet. It is marked on the General's part by a scramble for money and position, on his wife's by much inner turmoil. Historically Peggy stands in Arnold's shadow, but if their English autumn says anything to us at all, it says she was the stronger. Arnold had the power to act, to defy the stresses of business and the dangers of the battlefield; but Peggy had the power to endure. He could not cope with failure and disgrace. She could—and did.

Peggy Shippen had barely turned eighteen when in

CONTINUED ON PAGE 84

FACES FROM THE PAST-XXII

The session of Congress that opened on December 3, 1849, was regarded by men of the day as the most important ever held, for it was one that could well decide if the Union would endure. The unhappy factionalism caused by territorial expansion had come to a head over the question of California and whether it would be admitted as a free or slave state. Once again, the festering problem of slavery was out in the open, to arouse the worst passions of which the nation was capable. In this situation, the House of Representatives required three weeks and sixty-three ballots to elect a Speaker, and it was apparent that neither that body nor President Taylor was equal to the mounting crisis. The eyes of the country turned, as they had so often in recent years, to the Senate, and in particular to the great triumvirate of Daniel Webster, Henry Clay, and John C. Calhoun.

Clay, the most respected and beloved man in America, began the debate in January with an impassioned plea for moderation and compromise, and as he spoke, men watching John C. Calhoun wondered if the southerner would be able to rally his strength to reply. Wrapped in flannels, the Carolinian was "so pale and thin" that he "looked like a fugitive from the grave." Once he had been called a "cast-iron man who looks as if he had never been born and could never be extinguished," but for over a year now his health had been declining; he had fainted three times in the Senate lobby during the previous session, and these days he kept mostly to his room at Hill's boarding-house, in pain, racked with coughing, trying desperately to prepare for the ordeal ahead. During the last days of February, 1850, as the breaking point between North and South loomed closer, Calhoun decided that the only way he could present his views was to write them out and have an associate deliver the speech for him.

On Sunday, March 3, word flew through the capital that the South's great spokesman would come to the Senate chamber the following day for what must surely be his final appearance. Long before the session was called to order, "a brilliant and expectant audience" crowded the galleries and floor of the Senate, awaiting the grim, powerful southerner who was at the very apogee of his fame, the man one southern newspaper called "the moral and intellectual colossus of the age." Finally there was a stir at the door, and the great, gray-maned head of Calhoun was seen. A hush fell as he entered the chamber and was helped to his seat by friends. As he sank into it, his head was lowered in pain, and his bony, clawlike hands clutched the arms of the chair while he gathered his strength. Then he rose to his feet and stood erect, the wild eyes burning, the mouth a harsh slash across his jaw, and in a strong, clear voice he thanked the Senate for its courtesy, begging its indulgence while a colleague, James Mason of Virginia, read his speech. As Mason read, Calhoun sat "like a disembodied spirit," his long, black cloak pulled around him, his face drawn and white, and there were those who listened to his words who saw death written upon the South and upon the Union as it was on Calhoun's face. For it was immediately clear that he had no concessions to make, no compromise to offer. A realist, he knew that compromises are possible only between equals, and the South was no longer the equal of the North, either in economic or political strength.

His address traced the causes of the South's discontent, spoke of the growing concentration of power in the central government, described how the rights of the states had been swept away and control of the central government seized by the North, and bemoaned the fact that even spiritual ties between the sections—those represented by churches and political parties—were breaking up. Unless the North would concede the South equal rights in the new territories, he said, give up the fugitive slaves it was protecting, cease the "agitation of the slave question," and restore "the original equilibrium between the two sections," the North and South should agree to part in peace.

More than most of his contemporaries, Calhoun knew that time was running against the South; he perceived the significance of the North's population growth, of its material strength, of its deep popular feeling against any extension of slavery. In urging the South to secede, he was prompted by a belief that it must do so at once, acting while it had the strength to get out of the Union and stand alone. To compromise now was only to patch up the burning issue temporarily, for the Union could not endure, Calhoun argued, when the Constitution was used to defeat the very ends it was written to maintain. He believed that the goal of democracy is equity, not equality, and that it was not democracy when "fifty-one per cent of the people have a moral right to coerce forty-nine per cent." If popular majority became the ultimate law, he argued, the Constitution would be so much scrap paper.

Even as his last words were heard in the Senate, Calhoun knew that he had failed, and four weeks later, on March 31, he was dead. Bells tolled the news that the South's champion was gone, causing one man to observe that his philosophy had summed up "a whole people and a whole civilization." A similar thought crossed the mind of a Yankee soldier, some fifteen years later. As he stood amid the ruins of Charleston, South Carolina, and looked down upon Calhoun's tomb, it occurred to him that "the whole South is the grave of Calhoun." —*Richard M. Ketchum*

Reginald Rives, one of the most active members of the Coaching Club. He was its historian and in 1933 became its president. The painter, Richard Newton, Jr., appropriately placed an old English coaching scene in the background.

*In the last quarter of the nineteenth century you could ride
in a handsome coach-and-four from a fashionable hotel on Fifth Avenue
to Tuxedo Park or even to Philadelphia. The fare was just
three dollars, and your driver might be a Roosevelt or a Vanderbilt*

When the Coachman Was a Millionaire

By FRANK KINTREA

The annual report for the 1906 season of the New York-to-Ardsley run of the public coach *Pioneer,* operated by the Coaching Club of New York, was both dismal and disconcerting. It showed a net deficit of $6,845.98, and while this was a slight improvement over the previous year (when the deficit had soared to $7,309.01), the seemingly inexplicable downward trend of passenger traffic had continued unabated. The amount derived from the sale of seats had declined to an all-time low of $1,863.

Coming at a time when storm signals for the panic of 1907 were already flying, the appearance of figures in red on a balance sheet was profoundly disturbing to the fiscally sensitive gentlemen who served on the club's executive committee. After hearing the report of the public-coach committee on February 7, 1907, they requested a more detailed report for consideration by the entire membership at a special meeting to be held on February 16. Ominously for the future of public coaching, it was to be held at the Metropolitan Club in New York, where J. P. Morgan the Elder had decreed the fate of so many faltering industrial enterprises over brandy and cigars.

Although there are many still living who can recall the Coaching Club's annual spring parade in Central Park, when it was the grand finale of the New York social season, coaching itself is now remembered chiefly in terms of a vague association with old English prints of jolly tavern scenes. Public coaching, as it was called when it was a flourishing anachronism in

Alfred G. Vanderbilt, the Commodore's great-grandson, put the last public coach on the road in 1907.

the latter part of the nineteenth century and the early years of the twentieth, is, on the other hand, now quite forgotten. It was one of those curious but artificial customs that suddenly drop into oblivion. Fortunately its story is inseparably linked with the history of the Coaching Club of New York and has been preserved in the club's annals. They furnish a droll and flickering insight into the lives of that very small group of Americans, born and bred to wealth and leisure, whose influence on the nation's social and economic life was so disproportionate to their numbers.

The Coaching Club was founded in 1875 by nine gentlemen who sought to emulate the revival in England of coaching as a sport, rather than as the somewhat disagreeable but sole means of getting from one place to another which it had been before there were railroads. The leading spirits were Colonel William Jay and Colonel DeLancey Astor Kane, two gentlemen of independent means and socially impeccable antecedents, who had been regaling their fellow members of the Knickerbocker Club with tales of their exploits in the mother country. Colonel Jay had driven in England with such noted whips as the Duke of Beaufort and the Marquis of Blandford, and his enthusiasm was so great that he bought and shipped to the United States the coach that the Marquis had driven as a public conveyance between London and Dorking. Colonel Kane had been the first American to put a public coach on the road in Great Britain, and when he brought his yellow road coach *Tally-ho* to New York in 1876, he became the pioneer of public coaching in this country by making a regularly scheduled run between the Hotel Brunswick on Madison Square and Arcularius' Hotel at Pelham Bridge in Westchester. The *Tally-ho* and its distinguished driver made such an impression on the general public that forever after all coaches-and-four have joyfully been called "tallyhos" by the unknowing.

In the original rules of the club, its stated purpose was simply "to encourage four-in-hand driving in America." The use of vehicles drawn by four horses was, of course, no novelty, either as a form of sumptuous display or as a practical means of transportation. Until the 1840's, when the extensive development of inland waterways and the rapid growth of railroads finally made them unprofitable, stagecoaches carrying mail and passengers had long been a feature of American life, and they remained so in the West until much later. But their use had never been developed on a scale comparable to that in England, where the roads and highways were far superior and where there was an abundance of snug, well-run inns and taverns to solace a tired traveller at the end of a hard day's run. In the heyday of coach travel in England, people set

TEXT CONTINUED ON PAGE 75
ILLUSTRATIONS CONTINUE ON FOLLOWING PAGES

New York to Lakewood—in Style

The supreme achievement for a Coaching Club member was to own and drive a public coach that ran regularly between fixed termini on an announced schedule and carried paying passengers. Among the fortunate few who achieved this aim was James Hazen Hyde. For six weeks in the spring of 1903 his coach *Liberty*—using changes of eleven teams of horses—ran between the Holland House on Fifth Avenue and the fashionable Hotel Laurel-in-the-Pines at Lakewood, New Jersey. The *Liberty* left New York at 9:00 A.M. on Tuesdays, Thursdays, and Saturdays and reached Lakewood, some seventy-nine miles away, at 6:10 P.M. Return trips left at 8:30 A.M. on Mondays, Wednesdays, and Fridays. The pleasures of this run were caught by the German-born artist Max Klepper in a series of twelve water colors commissioned by Hyde. Six of these are reproduced on the following pages. Hyde—who joined the Coaching Club in 1901—was one of its most flamboyant members. His father had amassed a fortune as founder of the Equitable Life Assurance Society, and after his death in 1899 young Hyde set out to cut a grand social figure. Two years after he drove the *Liberty* as a public coach, he gave a costume ball at Sherry's that was reported to have cost two hundred thousand dollars. This extravagance shook public confidence in insurance companies, and the heat from an official investigation into their finances forced Hyde to move the base of his revels to Paris. He lived in Europe much of the time until his death at eighty-three in 1959, and never put a coach on the road again.

James Hazen Hyde

Leaving the Holland House in New York City

Crossing the bridge near Turkey Blue Ball, New Jersey

Taking refreshments at Freehold

Changing horses at Squankum

Waiting for the Jersey Central to pass near Lakewood

Arriving at the Laurel-in-the-Pines, Lakewood

The Marianas

Japanese naval air power was wrecked at the Battle of the Philippine Sea, but, says a U.S. carrie

By June, 1944, the U.S. Navy had inflicted disastrous losses on the Japanese Imperial Navy and had seized control of the Central Pacific. The Gilbert and Marshall Islands had fallen; MacArthur's forces were pressing relentlessly up the Bismarck Archipelago toward Rabaul, which Navy fliers had battered so hard that they had renamed it Rubble; and, two months before, a surprise carrier attack had neutralized the Japanese stronghold of Truk. The stage was thus set for a decisive naval confrontation at the Mariana Islands, only 1,500 miles from Tokyo. The U.S. objective was to seize Saipan and Guam and, in the process, to lure the remainder of the Imperial Navy into a death battle. The Japanese rose to the bait, and in the resulting Battle of the Philippine Sea, the pilots of Admiral Marc A. Mitscher's Task Force 58 effectively destroyed Japan's carrier air power. Three Japanese carriers went to the bottom, but the rest of the enemy fleet fled out of Mitscher's attack range. The escape of these ships prompted a round of bitter debate between the Navy's "Gun Club," composed of battleship admirals like Raymond A. Spruance (Mitscher's commander during the Marianas operation), and the advocates of the fast carrier task forces. One such advocate is Admiral J. J. "Jocko" Clark, U.S.N. (Retired), an Oklahoma-born, part-Cherokee pioneer of naval aviation who commanded the new Yorktown before his promotion to rear admiral in 1944. Clark's battle record in World War II was aptly described by the Chief of Naval Operations, Admiral Chester W. Nimitz, when he introduced him to the 1945 American Legion Convention in Chicago as "the fightingest admiral of the fleet." Clark's proudest moment, however, came at a ceremony later that year when he received his second Distinguished Service Medal. As he presented Clark with the award, Admiral Mitscher called him "my best carrier task group commander." Jocko was one of Mitscher's four group commanders in the Battle of the Philippine Sea, and he now tells his version of that crucial engagement in the following excerpt from his book Carrier Admiral, soon to be published by David McKay Co.
—The Editors

26

U.S. NAVY

Turkey Shoot

admiral who was there, our Navy missed a chance to destroy the enemy fleet and shorten the war

By ADMIRAL J. J. CLARK

Task Force 58 sortied from its Marshall Islands bases on June 6, 1944, the landings on Saipan being scheduled for June 15. My Task Group 58.1 left Kwajalein to rendezvous with 58.2 (Rear Admiral A. E. Montgomery), 58.3 (Rear Admiral J. W. Reeves), and 58.4 (Rear Admiral W. K. Harrill), which came out of Majuro. Fueling took two days, June 8 and 9. On the night of the eighth, our radar registered several "bogies"—enemy search planes—but they never made contact with our force. "Snoopers" began to approach our combat air patrol on the tenth. Fighter director Charles D. Ridgway dispatched a group of Hellcats to destroy them before they could sight the force and radio back our position to their base. We shot down the first snooper forty-seven miles from the task group, and a few minutes later splashed another. Land-based Liberators from Eniwetok preceded the carriers; one of them shot down a Betty, but not before we overheard the pilot reporting our position. This incident prompted me to ask permission from Mitscher to station picket destroyers equipped with radar and fighter directors ahead of the group, with their own combat air patrol to detect enemy snoopers before they sighted the carriers. With Mitscher's approval, on the morning of June 11 I sent two destroyers fifty miles ahead of the force and a third one twenty-five miles. This precaution became standard procedure for the fast carriers and was greatly expanded later in the war.

Making excellent time from the Marshalls to the target area, Task Force 58 was attacked by long-range enemy patrol bombers on the morning of June 11. When the shooting started, I sent out a final word of encouragement to the men of my task group: "Message to all hands. We need no special incentive, but Guam belongs to us. Deliver every bomb and bullet where it will do the most good. . . . God be with you and good luck. S/S Admiral Clark." Our combat air patrol Hellcat pilots were the first to see action. During the morning and early afternoon, our new picket destroyers directed *Yorktown* fighters about forty miles beyond the force to shoot down six enemy patrol bombers, one of which yielded two survivors. I could not resist sending a signal to my old ship: "Your combat air patrol has turned in the usual and expected top-notch *Yorktown* performance. Congratulations."

Since Task Force 58 was already under attack from enemy air units based on the target islands, Admiral Mitscher realized that if we waited until the next day for our customary predawn fighter sweep, the force would be under constant attack during the night. To avoid that, and to catch the Japanese by surprise, we launched the fighter sweep on that very afternoon. At 1 P.M. we began launching from a position 192 miles east of Guam. *Hornet* and *Yorktown* each sent off sixteen Hellcats, while *Belleau Wood* and *Bataan* each launched twelve. In all, from Task Force 58, 212 F6F's and ten life-raft-laden bombers were included in the sweep.

The afternoon fighter sweep had indeed caught the Japanese unaware. Reeves and Harrill worked over Saipan and Pagan, Montgomery hit Tinian, and I took Guam and Rota. Lieutenant Commander William A. Dean, skipper of Fighting 2 from the flagship, led the Hellcats into their strafing and bombing runs, which pitted the airstrips and destroyed several parked planes. The thirty Zeros that appeared were quickly engaged and shot down. Though antiaircraft fire was heavy, our planes easily carried the day. I signalled the ships in the task group: "Damn well done. Upwards of thirty airborne aircraft destroyed against one of ours shot down." In all, about 150 Japanese planes were destroyed by Task Force 58 at the cost of eleven Hellcats; three of our pilots were rescued. The total score for my task group on that day was forty-one enemy planes shot down. That night and the next morning no planes molested Task Force 58.

The customary pre-invasion destruction of enemy positions and equipment on the target islands began on June 12. Japanese antiaircraft gunners, lying in wait for our bombers and fighters, threw up a fire so withering that Fighting 24 from *Belleau Wood* reported it as "the heaviest encountered by this squadron in its nine months of combat experience." At dawn I sent out search planes 325 miles to the southwest to look for enemy warships; they sighted a convoy of six small Japanese vessels, destroyers and transports, about 270 miles west of Guam, heading south at eight knots. We launched a special strike against this convoy, but our

"Jocko" Clark on the Hornet's *bridge*

planes failed to relocate it. I had the bombers drop their bombs on Guam as they returned. To conclude the day's operations, *Hornet*'s planes dropped leaflets to the Chamorro natives on Guam announcing our intention to free them from Japanese domination.

Before daylight next morning, we launched another search-strike to look for that convoy. Two radar-equipped night fighters led twenty Hellcats from *Hornet* and *Yorktown*, followed by two rescue-equipped SB2C dive bombers. Each fighter carried one five-hundred-pound bomb. Finally the convoy was sighted and the planes attacked it, but the fighter pilots were inexperienced in the art of bombing warships and succeeded in damaging only one. Also, the 350-mile range was the longest carrier air strike of record at that time. Our other planes pounded Guam and were joined by the surface ships. By the end of that day, no aircraft remained on Guam that could possibly assist the defenders of Saipan when that island was assaulted two days later.

During the morning of June 13, Captain W. K. "Sol" Phillips, my screen commander and the skipper of the cruiser *Oakland,* had sent me a signal regarding Tokyo Rose, the infamous American-born Japanese woman broadcaster: "Tokyo Rose has just announced on the radio that all our ships are sunk."

I signalled back: "Do not believe Tokyo Rose. When the rising sun goes down she will sing a different song." This message began an exchange between Phillips and me referring to Tokyo Rose; thereafter, signalmen in my task group kept on the lookout for the Tokyo Rose messages to pass along to their friends.

During the attacks on Guam, Lieutenant (j.g.) Beath and his radio interceptors had been picking up Japanese radio transmissions and decoding messages relating to aircraft movements. We learned that the Japanese were sending great numbers of planes from the home islands to Chichi Jima and Iwo Jima, about seven hundred miles to the north, for attacks on our shipping off Saipan. Mitscher had the same messages confirmed by our submarines in the area. He wanted these planes destroyed.

Mitscher sent Harrill and me north to stop this buildup and to knock out the airfields in the "Jimas." On June 14, as our two groups rendezvoused, I received a message from Harrill saying that he did not want to go north to hit the Jimas. I could not believe he meant it, so I had Douglas "Tex" McCrary, my air operations officer, fly

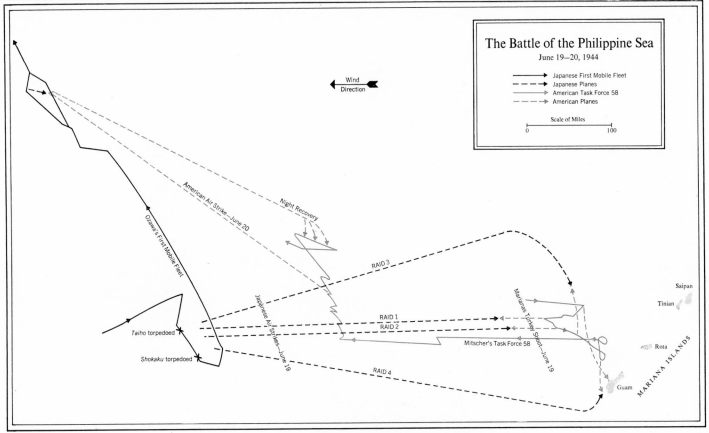

The Battle of the Philippine Sea
June 19—20, 1944

→ Japanese First Mobile Fleet
- - → Japanese Planes
→ American Task Force 58
- - → American Planes

Scale of Miles
0 — 100

Wind Direction

Ozawa's First Mobile Fleet

American Air Strike—June 20

Night Recovery

RAID 3

RAID 1
RAID 2

Japanese Air Strikes—June 19

Taiho torpedoed

Shokaku torpedoed

RAID 4

Marianas Turkey Shoot—June 19

Mitscher's Task Force 58

Saipan

Tinian

Rota

MARIANA ISLANDS

Guam

The unbroken red lines on this battle map demonstrate how Task Force 58 was kept cruising on the defensive near Guam during the so-called Turkey Shoot on June 19, while Admiral Ozawa's Mobile Fleet maneuvered beyond our combat air range. Not until the following day were Mitscher's swift carriers turned loose after the retreating enemy ships, and by then pursuit was at extreme range. The jagged lines at center indicate where our carriers turned back into the wind to launch aircraft, which on June 20 sank the carrier Hiyo.

me over to Harrill's flagship, *Essex,* for a talk. Harrill was firm in his desire not to go north at all. He said heavy weather was going to cover the Jimas and that the Japanese fleet might come out from the Philippines to attack the shipping off Saipan. His reluctance to carry out orders surprised me. Formerly a topflight officer, he seemed to have lost his zip.

Mitscher's order to Harrill and me was unusual. It was a multiple-address dispatch giving the two task groups the mission of striking the Jimas while remaining "tactically concentrated." Ordinarily the senior officer would lead such an assignment, but neither of us was in tactical command. Later I learned that Mitscher had purposely written the order that way to give me freedom of action. Harrill's chief of staff, Captain H. E. "Blackie" Regan, and I spent hours trying to convince Harrill of the importance of stopping the Japanese air threat from the north. Exasperated, I finally said, "If you do not join me in this job, I will do it all myself." After that remark he agreed to participate, but he provided only token assistance. Nevertheless, seven carriers were better than four, and though concerned about Harrill, I returned to my flagship satisfied.

Our plans were to hit the Jimas for two days, June

16 and 17, and then to rejoin Mitscher off Saipan. That night, June 14, Spruance sent to Task Force 58 an important dispatch announcing that the Japanese fleet had left its anchorage at Tawi Tawi in the southern Philippines, presumably to prevent us from capturing the Marianas, and therefore we should shorten our strikes to just one day and hasten back to rejoin Mitscher for a possible fleet engagement. I calculated that two days were needed to destroy the enemy air strength at Chichi and Iwo Jima, so I speeded up my group to twenty-five knots to get us within aircraft range of the target one day early. This still gave us the two days of air strikes against the enemy.

When my task group reached a position 135 miles from Iwo Jima on the afternoon of the next day, we launched planes from my four carriers. They shot

CONTINUED ON PAGE 92

SMITHSONIAN INSTITUTION; PLATE COURTESY DIAL PRESS FROM *George Catlin and the Old Frontier*, BY HAROLD MC CRACKEN, 1959

O-KEE-PA

*In words and pictures, George Catlin recorded the secret ceremony,
a blend of mysticism and horrific cruelty, by which
the Mandans initiated their braves and conjured the life-sustaining buffalo*

The degree of physical torture to which some American Indians voluntarily submitted as part of their religious tradition appeared cruel and sanguinary to the few white men who witnessed such rites. An outstanding example, unknown to most readers of history because of the white man's general neglect of Indian customs and folklore, was the O-kee-pa ceremony by which the Mandans initiated fledgling warriors and summoned the all-important buffaloes. The tribe was very nearly exterminated in 1837 by one item for which white traders did not charge: smallpox. Fortunately, from a historical standpoint, the famous artist George Catlin visited the Mandans in their earth-lodge villages in what is now North Dakota before the disease decimated them; he left a record, in words and on canvas, of this remarkable ceremony. Catlin spent most of the summer of 1832 with the Mandans and, through a series of fortuitous circumstances, became the first white man to view the secret rites in their entirety. While the experience was fresh in his mind, Catlin wrote a description of it for a New York newspaper. Nine years later he

Opposite: Catlin's portrait of Mah-to-he-ha so impressed the Mandan medicine man that he invited him to witness the secret rites, in which the medicine man played O-kee-pa-ka-see-ka, the conductor of the ceremonies. At right is the feared Evil Spirit, from whom the women of the tribe symbolically seized the "power" to lure the buffalo herds.

included an expanded, illustrated version in his impressive survey of North American Indians. Then, in 1856, there appeared a scholarly tome, printed with congressional funds and edited by Henry Rowe Schoolcraft, in which a former Indian trader, Colonel David D. Mitchell, accused Catlin of having imagined the whole ceremony. Catlin, in France at the time trying to recoup his sagging personal fortune, immediately began to accumulate corroborating testimony, including a letter from Prince Maximilian of Wied-Neuwied, who had spent some time with the Mandans shortly after Catlin's visit (see "Carl Bodmer's Unspoiled West" in the April, 1963, AMERICAN HERITAGE). Catlin published *O-kee-pa*, complete with these testimonials, thirteen chromolithographs, and a fuller text, in 1867. But the rehabilitation of his reputation did not really begin until a few months after his death in 1872, when Joseph Henry, secretary of the Smithsonian Institution, included a strong defense of Catlin in his annual report. Since then, in the words of the Smithsonian's senior ethnologist, John C. Ewers, "Catlin's *O-kee-pa* has ripened into a nineteenth-century classic in the ethnology of western North America." His evaluation introduces the centennial republication of *O-kee-pa* by the Yale University Press. Excerpts begin overleaf. For another view of Indian spirituality, see "Reading, Writing, and History," page 80. —*The Editors*

YALE UNIVERSITY LIBRARY

During the summer of 1832 I made two visits to the tribe of Mandan Indians, all living in one village of earth-covered wigwams, on the west bank of the Missouri River, eighteen hundred miles above the town of St. Louis.

Their numbers at that time were between two and three thousand, and they were living entirely according to their native modes, having had no other civilized people residing amongst them or in their vicinity, that we know of, than the few individuals conducting the Missouri Fur Company's business with them, and living in a trading-house by the side of them....

The Mandans, in their personal appearance, as well as in their modes, had many peculiarities different from the other tribes around them. In stature they were about the ordinary size; they were comfortably, and in many instances very beautifully clad with dresses of skins. Both women and men wore leggings and moccasins made of skins, and neatly embroidered with dyed porcupine quills. Every man had his "tunique and manteau" of skins, which he wore or not as the temperature prompted; and every woman wore a dress of deer or antelope skins, covering the arms to the elbows, and the person from the throat nearly to the feet.

In complexion, colour of hair, and eyes, they generally bore a family resemblance to the rest of the American tribes, but there were exceptions, constituting perhaps one-fifth or one-sixth part of the tribe, whose complexions were nearly white, with hair of a silvery-grey from childhood to old age, their eyes light blue, their faces oval, devoid of the salient angles so strongly characterizing all the other American tribes and owing, unquestionably, to the infusion of some foreign stock.

Amongst the men, practised by a considerable portion of them, was a mode peculiar to the tribe, and exceedingly curious—that of cultivating the hair to fall, spreading over their backs, to their haunches, and oftentimes as low as the calves of their legs; divided into flattened masses of an inch or more in breadth, and filled at intervals of two or three inches with hardened glue and red or yellow ochre....

The Mandans (*Nu-mah-ká-kee,* pheasants, as they called themselves) have been known from the time of the first visits made to them to the day of their destruction, as one of the most friendly and hospitable tribes on the United States frontier; and it had become a proverb in those regions, and much to their credit ... "that no Mandan ever killed a white man."

I was received with great kindness by their chiefs and by the people, and afforded every facility for making my portraits and other designs and notes on their customs; and from Mr. [James] Kipp, the conductor of the Fur Company's affairs at that post, and his interpreter, I was enabled to obtain the most complete interpretation of chiefly all that I witnessed.

I had heard, long before I reached their village, of their "annual religious ceremony," which the Mandans call "*O-kee-pa.*" ... I resolved to await its approach, and in the meantime, while inquiring of one of the chiefs whose portrait I was painting, when this ceremony was to begin, he replied that "it would commence as soon as the willow-leaves were full grown under the bank of the river."...

As I have before said, these people all lived in one village, and their wigwams were covered with earth—they were all of one form; the frames or shells constructed of timbers, and covered with a thatching of willow-boughs, and over and on that, with a foot or two in thickness, of a concrete of tough clay and gravel, which became so hard as to admit the whole group of inmates, with their dogs, to recline upon their tops. These wigwams varied in size from thirty to sixty feet in diameter, were perfectly round, and often contained from twenty to thirty persons within.

The village was well protected in front by a high and precipitous rocky bank of the river; and, in the rear, by a stockade of timbers firmly set in the ground, with a ditch inside, not for water, but for the protection of the warriors who occupied it when firing their arrows between the pickets....

The *"Medicine Lodge,"* the largest in the village and seventy-five feet in diameter, with four images (sacrifices of different-coloured and costly cloths) suspended on poles above it, was considered by these people as a sort of temple, held as strictly sacred, being built and used solely for these four days' ceremonies, and closed during the rest of the year.

In an open area in the centre of the village stands the Ark (or *"Big Canoe"*), around which a great proportion of their ceremonies was performed. This rude symbol, of eight or ten feet in height, was constructed of planks and hoops, having somewhat the appearance of a large hogshead standing on its end, and containing some mysterious things which none but the *medicine men* were allowed to examine. An evidence of the sacredness of this object was the fact that though it had stood, no doubt for many years, in the midst and very centre of the village population, there was not the slightest discoverable bruise or scratch upon it! ...

The *O-kee-pa,* though in many respects apparently

so unlike it, was strictly a *religious ceremony*, it having been conducted in most of its parts with the solemnity of religious worship, with abstinence, with sacrifices, and with prayer, whilst there were three other distinct and ostensible objects for which it was held.

1st. As an annual celebration of the event of the "subsiding of the waters" of the Deluge, of which they had a distinct tradition, and which in their language they called *"Mee-ne-ró-ka-há-sha"* (the settling down of the waters).

2nd. For the purpose of dancing what they called *"Bel-lohk-na-pick"* (the bull dance), to the strict performance of which they attributed the coming of buffaloes to supply them with food during the year.

During the O-kee-pa the Mandan spectators filled the central square and lodge roofs to witness the bull dances. Eight men wearing buffalo skins performed several times each day around the cylindrical "Big Canoe" at center. The Evil Spirit (shown entering from the left foreground) appeared on the fourth day; his defeat before the magic power of the tribe's medicine man traditionally ensured an abundant hunting season. The four grotesqueries suspended on poles above the guarded entrance to the sacred medicine lodge are tribal sacrifices to the Great Spirit. Catlin described them as consisting of "ten or fifteen yards of blue and black cloth each, purchased from the Fur Company at fifteen to twenty dollars per yard, which are folded to resemble human figures, with eagle feathers on their heads and masks on their faces."

33

3rd. For the purpose of conducting the young men who had arrived at the age of manhood during the past year, through an ordeal of privation and bodily torture, which, while it was supposed to harden their muscles and prepare them for extreme endurance, enabled their chiefs, who were spectators of the scene, to decide upon their comparative bodily strength and ability to endure the privations and sufferings that often fall to the lot of Indian warriors, and that they might decide who amongst the young men was the best able to lead a war party in an extreme exigency.

The season having arrived for the holding of these ceremonies, the leading *medicine* (mystery) man of the tribe presented himself on the top of a wigwam one morning before sunrise, and haranguing the people told them that "he discovered something very strange in the western horizon, and he believed that at the rising of the sun a great white man would enter the village from the west and open the *Medicine Lodge*."

In a few moments the tops of the wigwams, and all other elevations, were covered with men, women, and children on the look-out; and at the moment the rays of the sun shed their first light over the prairies and back of the village, a simultaneous shout was raised, and in a few minutes all voices were united in yells and mournful cries. . . .

All eyes were at this time directed to the prairie, where, at the distance of a mile or so from the village, a solitary human figure was seen descending the prairie hills and approaching the village in a straight line, until he reached the picket, where a formidable array of shields and spears was ready to receive him. A large body of warriors was drawn up in battle-array, when their leader advanced and called out to the stranger to make his errand known, and to tell from whence he came. He replied that he had come from the high mountains in the west, where he resided—that he had come for the purpose of opening the *Medicine Lodge* of the Mandans, and that he must have uninterrupted access to it, or certain destruction would be the fate of the whole tribe.

The head chief and the council of chiefs, who were at that moment assembled in the council-house, with their faces painted black, were sent for, and soon made their appearance in a body at the picket, and recognized the visitor as an old acquaintance, whom they addressed as *"Nu-mohk-múck-a-nah"* (the *first* or *only* man). All shook hands with him, and invited him within the picket. He then harangued them for a few minutes, reminding them that every human being on the surface of the earth had been destroyed by the water excepting himself, who had landed on a high mountain in the West, in his canoe, where he still resided, and from whence he had come to open the *Medicine Lodge,* that the Mandans might celebrate the subsiding of the waters and make the proper sacrifices to the water, lest the same calamity should again happen to them.

The next moment he was seen entering the village under the escort of the chiefs, when the cries and alarms of the villagers instantly ceased, and orders were given by the chiefs that the women and children should all be silent and retire within their wigwams, and their dogs all to be muzzled during the whole of that day, which belonged to the Great Spirit.

. . . I had a fair view of the reception of this strange visitor from the West; in appearance a very aged man, whose body was naked, with the exception of a robe made of four white wolves' skins. His body and face and hair were entirely covered with white clay, and he closely resembled, at a little distance, a *centenarian* white man. In his left hand he extended, as he walked, a large pipe, which seemed to be borne as a very sacred thing. The procession moved to the *Medicine Lodge,* which this personage seemed to have the only means of opening. He opened it, and entered it alone, it having been (as I was assured) superstitiously closed during the past year, and never used since the last annual ceremony.

The chiefs then retired to the council-house, leaving this strange visitor sole tenant of this sacred edifice; soon after which he placed himself at its door, and called out to the chiefs to furnish him "four men,—one from the *North,* one from the *South,* one from the *East,* and one from the *West,* whose hands and feet were clean and would not profane the sacred temple while labouring within it during that day."

These four men were soon produced, and they were employed during the day in sweeping and cleaning every part of the temple, and strewing the floor, which was a concrete of gravel and clay, and ornamenting the sides of it, with willow boughs and aromatic herbs which they gathered in the prairies, and otherwise preparing it for the *"Ceremonies,"* to commence on the next morning.

During the remainder of that day, while all the Mandans were shut up in their wigwams, and not allowed to go out, *Nu-mohk-múck-a-nah* (the *first* or *only* man) visited alone each wigwam, and, while crying in front of it, the owner appeared and asked, "Who's there?" and "What was wanting?" To this *Nu-mohk-múck-a-nah* replied by relating the destruction of all the human family by the *Flood,* excepting himself, who had been saved in his "Big Canoe," and now dwelt in the West; that he had come to open the *Medicine Lodge,* that the Mandans might make the necessary sacrifices to the water, and for this purpose it was requisite that he should receive at the door of every Mandan's wigwam some edged tool to be given to the water as a sacrifice, as it was with such tools that the *"Big Canoe"* was built.

He then demanded and received at the door of every Mandan wigwam, some edged or pointed tool or instrument made of iron or steel, which seemed to have been procured and held in readiness for the occasion; with these he returned to the *Medicine Lodge* at evening, where he deposited them, and where they remained during the four days of the ceremony. . . .

Nu-mohk-múck-a-nah rested alone in the Medicine Lodge during that night, and at sunrise the next morning, in front of the lodge, called out for all the young men who were candidates for the *O-kee-pa* graduation as warriors, to come forward—the rest of the villagers still enclosed in their wigwams.

In a few minutes about fifty young men, whom I learned were all of those of the tribe who had arrived at maturity during the last year, appeared in a beautiful group, their graceful limbs entirely denuded, but without exception covered with clay of different colours from head to foot—some white, some red, some yellow, and others blue and green, each one carrying his shield of bull's hide on his left arm, and his bow in his left hand, and his *medicine bag* in the right.

In this plight they followed *Nu-mohk-múck-a-nah* into the Medicine Lodge in "Indian file," and taking their positions around the sides of the lodge, each one hung his bow and quiver, shield and *medicine bag* over him as he reclined upon the floor of the wigwam.

Nu-mohk-múck-a-nah then called into the *Medicine Lodge* the principal *medicine man* of the tribe, whom he appointed *O-kee-pa-ka-see-ka* (Keeper or Conductor of the Ceremonies), by passing into his hand the large pipe which he had so carefully brought with him, "which had been saved in the big canoe with him," and on which it will appear the whole of these mysteries hung.

Nu-mohk-múck-a-nah then took leave of him by

PLATE COURTESY DIAL PRESS FROM *George Catlin and the Old Frontier*, BY HAROLD MC CRACKEN, 1959

shaking hands with him, and left the Medicine Lodge, saying that he would return to the West, where he lived, and be back again in just a year to reopen the Medicine Lodge. He then passed through the village, shaking hands with the chiefs, and in a few moments was seen disappearing over the hills from whence he came the day previous. . . .

Here is the proper place to relate the manner in which I gained admission to this sacred temple . . . [which had] a double door, with an intervening passage and an armed sentinel at each end, positively denying all access except by permission of the Conductor of the Ceremonies, and strictly guarding it against the approach or gaze of women, who, I was told, had never been allowed to catch the slightest glance of its interior. . . . Luckily for me, I had completed a portrait the day before, of the renowned doctor or *"mystery*

UNIVERSITY MUSEUM, UNIVERSITY OF PENNSYLVANIA

man," to whom the superintendence of the ceremonies had just been committed, and whose vanity had been so much excited by the painting that he had mounted on to a wigwam with it, holding it up by the corners and haranguing the villagers, claiming that "he must be the greatest man among the Mandans, because I had painted his portrait before I had painted the great chief; and that I was the greatest *'medicine'* of the whites, and a great chief, because I could make so perfect a duplicate of him that it set all the women and children laughing!"

This man, then, in charge of the Medicine Lodge, seeing me with one of my men and Mr. Kipp, the fur trader, standing in front of the door, came out, and passing his arm through mine, politely led me into the lodge, and allowing my hired man and Mr. Kipp, with one of the clerks of his establishment, to follow. We took our seats, and were allowed to resume them on the three following days, occupying them most of the time from sunrise to sundown. . . .

The Conductor or Master of the Ceremonies then took his position, reclining on the ground near the fire, in the centre of the lodge, with the medicine pipe in his hand, and commenced crying, and continued to cry to the Great Spirit, while he guarded the young candidates who were reclining around the sides of the lodge, and for four days and four nights were not allowed to eat, drink, or to sleep.

By such denial great lassitude, and even emaciation, was produced, preparing the young men for the tortures which they afterwards went through.

The Medicine Lodge . . . presented the most strange and picturesque appearance. Its sides were curiously decorated with willow-boughs and aromatic herbs, and its floor (covered also with willow-boughs) with a curious arrangement of buffalo and human skulls.

There were also four articles of veneration and importance lying on the ground, which were sacks, containing each some three or four gallons of water. These seemed to be objects of great superstitious regard, and had been made with much labour and ingenuity, being constructed of the skins of the buffalo's neck, and sewed together in the forms of large tortoises lying on their backs, each having a sort of tail made of raven's quills, and a stick like a drumstick lying on it, with which, as will be seen in a subsequent

CONTINUED ON PAGE 69

Catlin was the first white man permitted inside the medicine lodge to view the torturous initiation of the young braves, who, debilitated by fasting, were brutally suspended from the lodge roof, then spun around by attendants with poles until they lost consciousness. Their ability to withstand pain, and the speed with which they revived, enabled the tribe's elders to select the leaders of future Mandan war parties.

At the Oak Bluffs pier (above) excursionists from the mainland could board a narrow-gauge railroad for a breezy ten-mile ride along the shores of Martha's Vineyard. But it was only a short walk from the pier to the island's main attraction: the retreat of the Methodist brethren (below).

OAK BLUFFS

Newport it was not; but to judge by its summertime throngs, its religious fervor, and the exuberance of its architecture, there was nothing to match the likes of the "Cottage City of America"

Ulysses S. Grant never said much during his brief stay at Oak Bluffs. He rode about in a carriage with Mrs. Grant, waving to the crowds; he watched the fireworks from a balcony at Dr. Tucker's cottage, and he attended Sunday services at the Methodist tabernacle. According to one of his pastors, he found his peace with God at that meeting, but Grant himself never said whether that was so, and nobody seemed disappointed. Nobody expected him to say much of anything. What really counted was that he, the President of the United States, was there, at Oak Bluffs, Massachusetts, on the island of Martha's Vineyard. And for anyone who likes to see the people of history make a highly appropriate entrance, even if only on a very small stage, it is a fine thing that he cruised over that August afternoon aboard Lincoln's old steamer, *River Queen*.

In the years just preceding Grant's visit, the carpenters of Martha's Vineyard had put aside all their no-nonsense, salt-box architectural heritage and, working with scroll saws and fresh pine shipped in from Maine, had built an entire town in that particular style later to be known as General Grant Gothic. There was, to be sure, plenty of gingerbread glory to be seen in other places—in Cape May, New Jersey, and in Sea Cliff and Chautauqua, New York—but Oak Bluffs was something else again. It was quite possibly the most joyous-looking little town in the land, all new and freshly painted, a fair-weather place of countless turrets and towers, fancy trimmed gables, stained glass, porches, balconies, and endless plank walks. It was, just as its publicity so proudly proclaimed, the Cottage City of America.

Twenty years earlier, before the war, Oak Bluffs had been only the site of a Methodist camp meeting. The brethren had been gathering there summers since 1835, pitching their tents in a grove of scrub oaks just back from some meager clay bluffs on the island's landward shore. But after the war more and more tents had been replaced by tiny cottages built almost exactly along the lines of the tents. (Often a cottage took several years to evolve from the tent, with board walls replacing canvas this summer, a porch being added the next, and so forth.) At the end of the eighteen sixties the real boom began. A great many other people besides the Methodists had by then discovered the island's charm, and the islanders recognized that the summer trade might well supplant their all but vanished whaling industry.

Within three or four years, hundreds of summer houses were built at Oak Bluffs, and unlike those across the way at Newport, these were truly "cottages." For all their elegant style—their grandeur, really—they were with few exceptions quite small in

 By DAVID G. McCULLOUGH

Inside a gigantic sailcloth tabernacle the faithful and the curious gathered twice daily. Outside among the trees a sign read: THE VINEYARD IS OUR RESTING PLACE—HEAVEN IS OUR HOME.

From such Gothic camping gear as this (seen on the day Grant arrived) hundreds of still more splendorous "wooden tents" had evolved by the 1870's. A cottage like the one at right cost about $600.

scale, modestly furnished, and remarkably inexpensive. The place was, as one man put it, "the delight of the middle classes." Through July and August, excursion steamers plowed back and forth from Boston, Providence, Hartford, Bridgeport, and New Bedford. Some days as many as twenty boats docked at the Oak Bluffs pier, sending upwards of five thousand people ashore. On weekends the town's population would swell to thirty thousand or more. By 1874, the year Grant stopped over, the Methodist campground with its monstrous new tent was the biggest camp meeting in the country and was still the heart of the town. But the rest of Oak Bluffs was a full-blown summer resort with its own less pious attractions: bathing, band concerts, boating, croquet, ice cream, and "promenading," which generally appeared first on lists of "things to do at Oak Bluffs." A roller-skating rink had been built, and a vast frame hotel, the Sea View, which looked like a fantasy palace and which offered accommodations (American plan) for $4.00 a day. Moreover, it was now possible to obtain a drink of whiskey, and slipping over the seven-foot fence that enclosed the campground had become a favorite after-curfew (10:00 P.M. sharp!) sport for some of the younger brethren.

But perhaps the greatest attraction of all was Oak Bluffs itself. Hundreds and hundreds of people came just to see the houses. Journalists came to look too. "A pretty style on the whole, and admirably adapted to its transitory uses," one of them said later. Another wrote: "The stranger when he first goes there is struck by its foreign and bizarre appearance, and yet it is not like any foreign place he has seen. . . . It is a sort of Mayfair of pleasure, a city of the night, which is unreal and insubstantial in its beauty and apparently as likely to pass away from sight any moment as the ships on the water horizon."

The houses were praised for their "diversity of style," for their gay colors, and for the way light played on their varied shapes and surfaces. Nearly everyone seemed to like them, and especially the way their design afforded the passer-by an easy view of domestic life inside. ("And still the view is more curious in the evening," wrote one visitor, "when every cottage is lighted, and the wide front doors, which open directly into the principal room, are thrown wide open, and the cottagers are sitting around inside or on the broad piazzas or balconies, and on gala evenings, when the fancy-colored Chinese lanterns are hung

TEXT CONTINUED ON PAGE 46

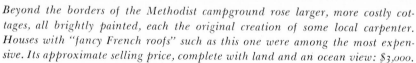

Beyond the borders of the Methodist campground rose larger, more costly cottages, all brightly painted, each the original creation of some local carpenter. Houses with "fancy French roofs" such as this one were among the most expensive. Its approximate selling price, complete with land and an ocean view: $3,000.

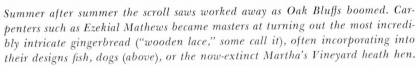

Summer after summer the scroll saws worked away as Oak Bluffs boomed. Car-
penters such as Ezekial Mathews became masters at turning out the most incredi-
bly intricate gingerbread ("wooden lace," some call it), often incorporating into
their designs fish, dogs (above), or the now-extinct Martha's Vineyard heath hen.

 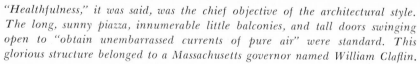

"Healthfulness," it was said, was the chief objective of the architectural style. The long, sunny piazza, innumerable little balconies, and tall doors swinging open to "obtain unembarrassed currents of pure air" were standard. This glorious structure belonged to a Massachusetts governor named William Claflin.

One of the grandest houses of all joined two identical campground cottages with a three-story tower from which, perhaps, one could look across the trees to blue water. By the eighties the building craze had fallen off. Oak Bluffs remained highly popular, but for the Vineyard carpenters a joyous heyday was over.

around on trees and cottages, the scene is really enchanting. . . .") There were some, of course, who had no such reaction. "The only substantial and satisfactory thing here is the sea that seems the greater for the weak things on its shore," wrote a Kentucky man. And within another generation, as tastes changed, the houses would be considered minor monstrosities.

Today a great part of Oak Bluffs still stands, and the Methodists still congregate in goodly numbers. But much of the gingerbread has been knocked off (often with the best intentions), and most of the houses look a good deal shabbier than those on the preceding pages. Still, one night a year lanterns are again strung through the campground, and the "Grand Illumination," as it has always been called, does not look much different than it did ninety years ago. There is still some talk of the time the President of the United States spent the night (the cottage where he stayed is still there, his room still furnished about as it was), and, encouragingly, there is a renewed appreciation for the architecture of the place. Then, too, there are some who claim that late on summer nights, when the old high-backed cane rockers tilt gently back and forth on Oak Bluffs porches, it is not the sea wind alone that makes them go.

David McCullough, an editor in the American Heritage Book Division, is a regular summer visitor to Martha's Vineyard. He wrote an account of the Johnstown Flood for our June, 1966, issue, and the research led subsequently to a book entitled The Johnstown Flood, *which will soon be published by Simon and Schuster.*

COLLECTION HOWARD C. WILSON

On August 28, 1874, all Oak Bluffs was elaborately bedecked in honor of the distinguished visitors pictured at right.

A memorable Oak Bluffs portrait shows President and Mrs. Grant (right) and their party (including Grant's former secretary, Orville Babcock) outside their gingerbread cottage.

death on the range

"I want my work to talk to the ordinary cowhand, as well as to experts who know a good deal about painting, in the same way that art of the Italian Renaissance talks to everyone." If Harry Jackson, the painter of the two pictures on these pages, had been shown this statement a dozen years ago and told that he himself would utter it in 1967, he would undoubtedly have laughed derisively. His reaction would not have been surprising, for in the late nineteen forties and early fifties, Harry Jackson was a member of that most un-Italian-Renaissance school of painting, Abstract Expressionism. Like many artists in the immediate postwar years, he had found traditional American painting dull and uninteresting and had turned elsewhere for inspiration, particularly to the French painter Matisse and the American drip-and-dribble master Jackson Pollock. His own work, brightly colored and fashionably abstract, had earned him two important exhibitions in New York and a leading critic's encomium: "most talented young painter in America." Yet as soon as success as a modernist was his, Harry

CONTINUED ON PAGE 83

The power of Harry Jackson as an interpreter of the West is evident in these two paintings. In The Stampede *(above) he has caught the terror of a rushing herd of longhorns— the dust-laden sky, the frantic efforts of the cowboys, the stumbling horse, the cowhand being dragged to his death.* The Range Burial *(right) captures a completely contrasting mood, one of silence and dignity, as the man killed in the stampede is laid in the earth.*

Pictures Worth a Second Look

Written history is fairly manageable stuff. The facts that are known can be artfully arranged to conceal those that are not known, or anyway to make them less noticeable. Awkward questions can be left unanswered just by leaving them unasked.

Historical photographs are quite another matter. The camera lens makes an instantaneous statement of fact, often a very comprehensive one. Elusive details that nobody present would otherwise have remembered, or would have agreed on if he had remembered, are caught at a single, irrefutable wink. There they are, quietly but stubbornly correcting the subjective impressions of partisan reporters; visual shards for the reconstruction of "what really happened."

Yet this sometimes leads to puzzles and surprises. It is a commonplace that ten minutes after an accident you can get ten different versions of the event, depending on whom you query; but if someone happened to take a photograph at just the right moment, you might think the facts would arrange themselves in a straightforward way. They don't always do so.

Whose grandfather IS that?

In the February AMERICAN HERITAGE, there was a story on Mayor Gaynor of New York, which included a prize-winning news photograph snapped at just the moment when Gaynor was shot by an irate citizen on the deck of a departing ocean liner in 1910. The person supporting Gaynor has been clearly identified as Benjamin C. Marsh, Secretary of the Committee on Congestion of Population for New York City (a committee, it may be remarked in passing, that should have

BROWN BROTHERS

Dr. George A. Smith   William Strauss   Robert Todd Lincoln

tried harder). Rushing up behind Gaynor is a stout, bearded gentleman who in that bewhiskered day might have been almost anybody's grandfather. With that thought in mind, consider the following photographs and excerpts from letters that arrived in our office after publication of the picture:

". . . I was wondering why your picture caption did not identify the man standing behind the wounded mayor? The man is Robert Todd Lincoln [Abraham Lincoln's eldest son], who had the uncanny habit of being around when people were shot at! . . . He was present . . . when Charles Guiteau shot President Garfield. In 1901 he was

among the guests who witnessed Leon Czolgosz shoot President McKinley."
Lloyd Ostendorf
Dayton, Ohio

". . . The picture was familiar to our family because the startled gentleman behind the Mayor was Mr. William Strauss, grandfather of my wife, née Elizabeth Strauss. . . ."
Rabbi W. Gunther Plaut
Toronto, Ontario

". . . Among those friends who had assembled [to wish Mayor Gaynor *bon voyage*] was my father, Dr. George Albert Smith. . . . As they came on deck, a waiting photographer approached the Mayor requesting his picture. . . . As the picture was about to be taken, shots rang out—the Mayor staggered—his secretary lunged to his side—and my father rushed forward, as the photograph reveals."
Susan Smith Reilly
New York City

Sympathetic but baffled, we dispatched a young lady to the New York Public Library to check the newspapers for August 10, 1910, and determine which one of these interesting claims was correct. She came back with the caption that was printed under the picture in the New York *World* on that date: "This photograph was taken by a *World* photographer an instant after Mayor Gaynor was shot. Supporting him is Benjamin C. Marsh. . . . Rushing to his assistance is Edward J. Litchfield, a Brooklyn neighbor of the Mayor."

Are there any other candidates?

"Strictly between us, you're sweeter than Venus . . ."

An even greater puzzle has grown out of—we choose the expression carefully, as will be seen in a moment—our frontispiece photograph in the June, 1967, issue. The focus of interest here, of course, is the succulent one-piece bathing beauty being surveyed by the celebrated Earl Carroll as part of the contest for the title of The Modern Venus. Although various members of our staff examined this picture with much care and enthusiasm, not a single editorial eye noticed a peculiarity since drawn to our attention by several letters from readers who must have looked at the whole thing more objectively than we did. Here is one such letter:

"I found the picture series on the 1931 'birdwatchers' and 'birds' in the June '67 issue amusing and nostalgic. One thing mystified me, however.

While glancing at the picture of the erstwhile bathing beauties, I noticed that there was a feminine left forearm seeming to spring forth from the brow of Earl Carroll and grasp the vertical shaft of the scales' height-measuring device. As far as I can tell there is no body in the photograph to which the forearm should properly belong.

Trick photography? Optical illusion?

Perhaps it belongs to one of the Coney Island ghosts I heard about during my boyhood in Brooklyn!"

Robert Simon
Longmeadow, Massachusetts

Well, we went back to our picture source to see if there was any sign of trick photography or fancy dodging in the darkroom: there was none. So far, in addition to Mr. Simon's suggestion about ghosts, it has been proposed that the arm obviously belongs to Venus herself, who in the tradition of Greek goddesses is indeed emerging full-blown from the brow of Earl Carroll, twentieth-century Zeus of female pulchritude; or that, alternatively, the arm is one of the two notoriously missing from the Venus of Milo, here materialized in order to help measure the contenders for her name. Any other more or less reasonable speculations will be gratefully entertained.

WIDE WORLD

PHOTO BY NORMAN ALLEY

Panegyric for Panay

One picture that we published in a recent issue evoked special interest but luckily led to no puzzles. A photograph in the April AMERICAN HERITAGE showed an American seaman on the gunboat *Panay* firing at attacking Japanese planes with a Lewis gun. In his haste to reach his post, he had neglected to put on his trousers. Readers wanted to know the identity of this impetuous hero, and we are pleased to report that he was—and is

—Ernest R. Mahlmann, chief boatswain's mate at the time of the *Panay* incident. Mahlmann won the Navy Cross for his out-of-uniform performance; he is now retired and lives in Elmhurst, Long Island. This tribute to him, by Vaun Al Arnold, appeared in the *Bureau of Navigation Bulletin* shortly after the episode:

Commend me to that noble soul
Who, in the battle's heat,
Rushed to his post without his pants,
The bomber's dive to meet;
Who stood upon the rocking deck
In careless disattire,
With shirt tail flaunting in the breeze,
To deal out fire for fire.
Old Glory's color deepened
As she floated o'er this son—
The man who had no time for pants
But plenty for his gun.
Come, name a million heroes,
But to me there'll never be
A finer show of nerve and grit
On any land or sea—
Then dwell upon your epics;
Should you feel an urge for chants,
Recall the sinking Panay
And the gunner minus pants!

CANYONLANDS

*In the red-rock country of southeastern Utah is
a new national park, a quarter-million acres of silence, brilliant
color, and vistas unmatched anywhere on earth*

By ROBERT L. REYNOLDS

"The landscape everywhere, away from the river, is of rock—cliffs of rock, tables of rock, plateaus of rock, terraces of rock, crags of rock. . . . a whole land of naked rock, with giant forms carved on it: cathedral-shaped buttes, towering hundreds or thousands of feet, cliffs that cannot be scaled, and canyon walls that shrink the river into insignificance . . . and all highly colored—buff, gray, red, brown, and chocolate—never lichened, never moss-covered, but bare, and often polished." Thus nearly a century ago John Wesley Powell, the first white man to explore it extensively, described the remote corner of southeastern Utah which in 1964 became our thirty-second national park.

Canyonlands does not have the easy charm of other parks, with their lush forests, clear mountain lakes, and abundant wildlife. Its distinguishing qualities are emptiness, silence, and austere, massive beauty; the impression it leaves upon the visitor is one of awe. Yet its quarter-million acres of mesas, canyons, arches, and monoliths surrounding the confluence of the Green and Colorado rivers constitute a gigantic geology lesson, in glowing colors, unduplicated anywhere else on earth. Its ancient Indian dwellings, built under overhanging ledges at about the time of the Crusades and abandoned now for seven centuries, speak of the mysteries of the continent's aboriginal past. Its twisted junipers and piñon pines, with here and there an occasional clump of desert holly and a sudden, startling cactus blossom, testify to nature's

marvelous ability to survive in a stark and arid land.

The land was not always dry. Hundreds of millions of years ago it was submerged under water, first under a vast inland salt sea, and successively under fresher seas; in the lowest elevations of the park—in the canyons of the Colorado and the Green—marine fossils can still be found if one looks for them carefully (so, in other places, can dinosaur tracks and petrified logs from the moist, warm climate of a later era). As the seas dried up and as, in the slow course of geologic time, the land rose and sank and rose again, layers of mud, wind-borne sand, and silt covered the deposited salt. These solidified into sandstones and limestones of varying hues and differing degrees of hardness. Once the seas had dried up, the natural forces of erosion—wind and rain, snow and frost—began their long, patient work of sculpturing the fantastic spires, the standing rocks, and the great crenelated buttes that confront the eye at every turn. And through the rock the rivers—not only the two major streams but their tributaries, and the creeks and rivulets tributary to *them*—slowly cut their labyrinthine ways.

This, then, is how the canyon lands were created, and the creation is still going on. Each spring the waters of melting snows flow down from the surrounding mountains, deepening and quickening the erosive rivers; steady winds scour the uplands, filling the air with the faintly acrid odor of powdered rock; and the runoff from sudden thunderstorms rushes down the dry washes. One knows that the land will never be quite the same tomorrow as it was yesterday. The changes are miniscule, of course, too small to be measured, but one is aware that a delicate arch seen today will wear thin and fall of its own weight one day, even though the day may be thousands of years distant, while new arches and pinnacles are constantly forming. It is a land that induces long thoughts.

Opposite page: From Grandview Point, in the park's northern section, one looks down 1,000 feet to the White Rim and another 500 feet to the floor of Standing Rock Basin, filled with massive buttes and slender monoliths. The only sign of man is the jeep road visible at lower left, once used by cowboys and uranium hunters, now by park visitors.

Rivermen, Rustlers, and Uranium Hunters

John Wesley Powell was not the first white man to see the spectacular red-rock country of Utah and northern Arizona. Spanish padres had traversed its lower reaches in 1776, and from time to time trappers and mountain men had wandered through this trackless wilderness. In the mid-nineteenth century Mormon missionaries and settlers trickled southward from their base at Salt Lake City into "Dixie," as they called it, to preach to the aborigines and to till the isolated fertile valleys. About the same time, two army officers, Lieutenant Joseph C. Ives and Captain J. N. Macomb, explored various parts of the lower Colorado. But it was Powell, a determined, resourceful Civil War veteran who had lost his right arm at Shiloh and was known the rest of his life as "the Major," who left his mark upon the river and the canyon lands.

He led two expeditions down the Green from its upper reaches in Wyoming, past its junction with the Colorado, and then down the Colorado through the Grand Canyon, whence the river flows on to the Gulf of California. On each of the two expeditions—the first in 1869, the second in 1871—Powell and a handful of men, in small wooden boats powered only by oars and the current, covered nearly a thousand miles. They mapped the meandering rivers, named many of the canyons, climbed up to the rims with barometer in hand to measure elevations, and made notes on the area's geology. The first trip, when the tricky channels and dangerous white-water stretches were strange to them, almost ended in disaster. Boats repeatedly swamped in the rapids, spilling men, rations, and precious scientific instruments into the water. After more than three months on the river, Powell's men were discouraged and in rags, and their food supply was dwindling dangerously. Three of them gave up and, leaving their comrades, struck out over the mountains for civilization. They never made it: a party of Shivwits Indians, mistaking them for some other white men who had killed one of their women, murdered all three. Two days later Powell and the others reached the safety of a Mormon settlement. After the two river voyages the Major himself spent much of his time in Washington, D.C., but others under his direction completed the exploration and charting of the plateau country of southern Utah and of Arizona north and west of the Colorado. One of our last great wildernesses was finally mapped.

U. S. GEOLOGICAL SURVEY, PHOTO BY J. K. HILLERS

John Wesley Powell, conqueror of the Colorado River, with one of his Indian guides

The remoteness and aridity of the canyon lands precluded extensive settlement, however, and for the next seventy-five years—until after World War II—about the only permanent white inhabitants were a few farmers, an occasional prospector or small mine operator, and the ranchers who ran their stock on the high mesa pastureland, along the streams, and in the grassy areas or "parks" scattered among the canyons. (Not recorded by the census taker were a few transient residents, rustlers, and fugitive train-robbers seeking hideouts in the more inaccessible rock crannies; the Hollywood horse-operas that have been filmed in the area are not entirely without basis in fact.) Then, in the mid-1950's, came what is still remembered locally as the Great Uranium Boom. As always in a great mineral rush, a few men got rich, but most made nothing. Still, for a while, prospectors and land speculators were jammed cheek by jowl into whatever housing they could find (some even slept in packing cases), claims were bought and sold over a bottle of whiskey, and the sleepy little town of Moab—today the site of park headquarters—ballooned from a population of 1,000 to ten times that. When within a few years the uranium market became glutted, the balloon burst. But the boom had focused national attention on the area. The uranium men had extended the stockmen's trails and jeep roads into the inner fastnesses of the canyon lands, and, in the process, opened up the country to prospectors for other minerals like oil and potash. To conservationists it was becoming apparent that if this scenic wilderness were to be preserved for posterity it would have to be done soon. Bates Wilson, superintendent of nearby Arches National Monument, began sending requests to his Park Service superiors for the creation of a national park. In 1959 a preliminary survey was made and in 1961 Secretary of the Interior Stewart L. Udall himself came out from Washington and later returned for an extensive camping trip. He was so impressed that he began plugging for a large park of about a million acres.

That scared the mineral interests. In the end, the best the park's advocates could get was a bill, sponsored by Utah's Senator Frank Moss and Representatives David S. King and M. Blaine Peterson, setting aside an area of 257,640 acres shaped like an hourglass, with the confluence of the rivers near the waist. The bill was a compromise, but it saved the heart of the canyon lands.

Canyonlands is still a largely undeveloped park, but though it is difficult to get around in, the effort is richly rewarding. The northern portion (see map on pages 62–63), occupying the top of the hourglass and thrusting southward toward the apex of the triangle formed by the junction of the Green River on the west and the upper Colorado on the east, embraces three topographical levels. At the base of the inverted triangle is a 6,000-foot mesa, some 20,000 acres in extent, called the Island in the Sky. It sheers off on all sides into deep canyons and is connected to the rest of the "mainland" only by a forty-foot-wide neck across which cowboys once drove their stock, barricading the narrow trail behind them so that the grassy Island became a giant natural pasture from which the cattle could not stray. About 1,000 feet below the Island and clearly visible from its heights is another table of land, called the White Rim because its surface is of light gray, almost white, sandstone; this in turn overlooks the winding rivers, isolated stretches of which can be seen as they twist in and out of their canyons another 1,000 feet farther down.

The Colorado, once the Green has joined it, continues southwestward. The park does not extend very far west of the Green or the lower Colorado; most of the bottom half of its hourglass is what is known as the Needles District, so called because of the weirdly-shaped pinnacles of rock which abound there. In this region are the isolated, rock-rimmed meadowlands like Chesler Park, as well as many of the most significant Indian pictographs, petroglyphs, and dwellings. Here, too, most of the park's lovely, delicate arches can be found.

There is a vital distinction at Canyonlands between "four-wheel-drive" and "two-wheel-drive" roads. The latter can be navigated in modern, low-slung automobiles with automatic transmissions; the former are too narrow, too bumpy, too sandy, or too steeply graded (and, in places, all four) for any vehicles but specially equipped jeeps. The Island in the Sky can be reached by car, however, and this one-day trip is the best way to begin a tour of the park, for it offers the most comprehensive overall view.

From just north of Moab on U.S. 160, a twenty-three-mile highway, paved part of the way, leads across the neck and onto the Island, culminating in Grandview Point, a rock-strewn flat dotted with juniper and piñon pine. Overlooks along its edges give breath-taking views of the White Rim and, below it, Standing Rock (now renamed Monument) Basin, filled with the spires and cathedral-shaped buttes that awed Major Powell. Sheer cliffs layered like cakes clearly tell the story of the earth's formation: to look 2,000 feet down to the distant, green-brown rivers is to look backward in an instant over nearly two million centuries of geologic time. From here and from Dead Horse Point State Park, situated on a similarly isolated mesa nearby, one can see the rock layers formed during the Permian, Jurassic, and Triassic eras as much as 180 million years ago; the synclines (downfolds) and anticlines (upfolds) of the earth's crust can be seen along the massive cliffs. The colors range from white to chocolate through all the reds in the spectrum, and they are never quite the same from hour to hour: deep red in the early morning, lightening toward buff in the brilliance of midday, purpling in shadow as the sun's light fades.

Only an eagle or a mountain goat could traverse the wilderness of serrated rock that separates the Island in the Sky from the Needles District in the lower section of the park. The human visitor must retrace his route out to the main highway, drive south to a point above the town of Monticello, then turn west again—over a thirty-five-mile road, graded but unpaved—until he reaches the ranger station near Cave Spring. Until circulating roads are built within the park (they have been surveyed, but construction—estimated to cost $300,000 a mile—has not yet begun), this marks the end of the trail for the ordinary automobile. From here on one must travel on foot, on horseback, or in the jouncing cab of a jeep. Most greenhorns choose a jeep.

If you don't have your own—and even if you do, you had better be an experienced, steel-nerved driver—you have to rely upon one of the jeep guides licensed to take visitors to the more remote areas of the park. Their rates, regulated by the Utah Public Service Commission, are steep: twenty-five dollars a day for each adult passenger, half that for children under twelve. But the operating expenses—sky-high insurance rates and rapid depreciation of equipment—are also steep, and the guides furnish everything: meals, sleeping bags, and much expert information.

Plus, of course, an exciting ride. One road into beautiful Chesler Park, for example, leads over two hills which seem impossible for any wheeled vehicle to negotiate. The first is called Elephant Hill—possibly because only an elephant could be expected to climb it; the other is known, for good and sufficient reasons, as S.O.B. Hill. In places the "road" consists of sheer, slick sandstone, and rises at angles exceeding forty-five degrees; one jeep passenger, holding tightly to the dashboard on a downgrade, is reported to have complained: "If I'm sitting down, how come I'm standing on my head?" But the trip is rewarding: along the way are fascinating Indian pictographs, particularly row upon row of handprints drawn or sprayed on the

stone with liquefied vegetable dyes. Chesler Park, when one finally reaches it, is a revelation. Here the harshness of sand and barren rock disappears, replaced by a circular carpet of grass ringed about by fin-shaped canyons and the odd standing rocks which have given their name to the entire district. Some do indeed resemble needles, while others look like huge mushrooms and still others like totem poles or the stubby, upthrust fingers of ancient giants.

The trip to Chesler, like that to the Island in the Sky, occupies a full day, even without following the trails that lead north and west to the confluence of the rivers (right). But the region around the confluence —where the lighter-hued Green curves into the muddier Colorado—is worthwhile. Young Fred Dellenbaugh, who accompanied Major Powell on his second expedition, stood upon a promontory here, and over thirty years later he remembered it vividly: "Here was revealed a wide cyclorama that was astounding," he wrote. ". . . It was a marvellous mighty desert of bare rock, chiselled by the ages out of the foundations of the globe, fantastic, extraordinary, antediluvian, labyrinthian, and slashed in all directions by crevices; crevices wide, crevices narrow, crevices medium, some shallow, some dropping till a falling stone clanked resounding into the far hollow depths." The description is accurate, and the terrain has hardly changed in the intervening years. Powell named the region Sin-av-to-weap—"Spirit Land."

And the spirits of ancient men still seem to linger within the park. Seven centuries ago, cliff-dwelling Indians inhabited the canyons east of the Needles; more of them lived here, probably, than in any other region of Canyonlands, for here were arable land and a reliable water supply. Here, too, the sandstone cliffs that border the tiny streams had eroded in such a way as to create alcoves, overhangs, and ledges suitable for the kind of houses the cliff-dwellers favored. Modern Indians know these ancient people only as "the old ones," but extensive archeological "digs" in recent years—including careful examination of their pottery, pictographs, slab-and-mortar houses, and sunken ceremonial chambers—have identified them as part of the Mesa Verde branch of the San Juan Anasazi. They were farmers of the late Pueblo II–early Pueblo III period who came into the Canyonlands area about the year 1075, subsisted on the corn and squash they raised and on whatever game they could bring down with their stone-tipped weapons, and vanished about 1275, probably driven away by a prolonged drought. Some of their dwellings, like Tower Ruin in Horse Canyon (opposite page), are still in reasonably good condition after seven hundred years.

The heart of the park, hedged by high buttes, is the confluence of the Green (right) and Colorado rivers.

Indians of several cultures left their drawings on "Newspaper Rock," near the park's southeast entrance. Tower Ruin (opposite page) is a relic of the cliff dwellers who lived in the area from about 1075 to 1275.

Overleaf: Paul Bunyan's Potty is one of many beautiful natural arches that have been carved by wind and water from Cedar Mesa sandstone.

Top: Looking across the broad and placid upper Colorado River toward the Island in the Sky area
Above: Sunrise on Junction Butte, a 6,400-foot formation located in the midsection of the park
Right: Chesler Park, a 500-acre meadow encircled by "Needles," looks like a natural Stonehenge.
Overleaf: A map of the Canyonlands area by the late David Greenspan shows the park boundaries as a dotted line. Grandview Point, almost at dead center, overlooks Junction Butte, Standing Rock Basin, and the White Rim. To the south and west is the confluence of the Colorado (right) and the Green (left). Chesler Park is below, to the right of the fold. The principal arches and Indian ruins lie near the park's extremities at lower right.

From the Island in the Sky the canyon lands are seen from the top down, as it were. But to float along the rivers (left) and see them from the bottom up as Powell and Dellenbaugh did, is a unique experience. Nowadays the park visitor may take a boat along the Green from Green River, Utah (considerably south of the Wyoming town of the same name that was Powell's jumping-off place), to a point a little below the confluence. Or one can cruise down the Colorado from Moab by jet boat to the same spot. That is as far as the jet boats can go; thereafter the river plunges into dangerous Cataract Canyon.

The upper rivers, relatively placid and shallow, meander through gorges of unbelievable grandeur. There are glimpses of beauty unexpected in a harsh, dry land. Suddenly, along the bank, a beach appears, its pure-white sand unmarked by human footprints. A flock of snipe or a rare blue heron is startled into flight by the buzz of the jet. In a fringe of cottonwood or tamarisk, deer, foxes, and bobcats can be seen.

Together the high mesas, the Needles and arches and cliff dwellings, and the rivers make this new national park a memorable wilderness experience. Park officials hope they can keep it so, even when—once the development work is completed—the expected flood of vacationers arrives. The planned circulating roads will never take the visitor everywhere in the park, and the rangers hope they will not be forced to expand the campgrounds beyond what the land's natural contours dictate. "Come to our wilderness," Superintendent Bates Wilson told a journalist not long ago, "but be ready to rough it."

Devils Garden

ARCHES NATIONAL MONUMENT

Delicate Arch

Double Arch

RT U.S.160

Park Avenue

Tower of Babel

MOAB

Dead Horse Pt

KANE SPRING CANYON

HATCH PT

Colorado River

HART BASIN

Standing Rock Basin

RUSTLER CANYON

Indian Creek

HARTS DRAW

Elephant Hill

SQUAW FLAT

Cave Spring

North Sixshooter Pk

LOST CANYON

Salt Creek

South Sixshooter Pk

esler Park

Druid Arch

Tower Ruin

Virginia Park

HORSE CANYON

DAVIS CANYON

THE NEEDLES

Angel Arch

East Fork

West Fork

CAMPGROUND
PRIMITIVE CAMPGROUND

A mysterious phenomenon, to which professional critics are usually oblivious, reoccurs often in the literary history of the United States. A man or a woman with no special talent for poetry will put together some apparently run-of-the-mill stanzas and manage to get them printed in a newspaper or magazine. The poem is read and talked about. It is reprinted here and there. People cut it out to carry in a billfold, or pin on a bulletin board, or put under the glass top of a desk, or frame and hang on a wall. Thousands memorize it. Eventually it becomes so well known—inexplicably, and often to the author's own amazement—that it is hard to find a literate person who has not read it. "Casey at the Bat" is such a poem, and its author, Ernest Lawrence Thayer, is a prize specimen of the one-poem poet. He wrote nothing else of merit. No one imagines that "Casey" is great in the sense that the poetry of Shakespeare or Dante is great; a comic ballad obviously must be judged by different standards. One doesn't criticize a slice of superb apple pie because it fails to taste like crepes suzette. Thayer was only trying to write a comic ballad, with clanking rhymes and a vigorous beat, that could be read quickly, understood at once, and laughed at by any newspaper reader who knew baseball. Somehow, in harmony with the curious laws of humor and popular taste, he managed to produce the nation's best-known piece of comic verse— a ballad that began a native legend as colorful and permanent as that of Johnny Appleseed or Paul Bunyan. Here, in time for the World Series, is Casey's story.

Casey at the bat

By MARTIN GARDNER

The man who made "Casey" famous was William DeWolf Hopper, shown in typical declaiming stance. Although Hopper was a comedian and a singer, he is now remembered mainly for his lively, colorful recitation of "Casey."

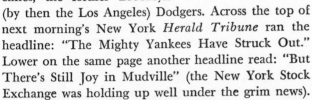

CULVER

One of the most humiliating defeats in the history of the New York Yankees took place on Sunday, October 6, 1963. Because a well-thrown ball bounced off the wrist of first baseman Joe Pepitone, the Yanks lost the fourth straight game and the World Series to their old enemies, the former Brooklyn (by then the Los Angeles) Dodgers. Across the top of next morning's New York *Herald Tribune* ran the headline: "The Mighty Yankees Have Struck Out." Lower on the same page another headline read: "But There's Still Joy in Mudville" (the New York Stock Exchange was holding up well under the grim news).

Every reader of those headlines knew that they came straight out of that immortal baseball ballad, that masterpiece of humorous verse, "Casey at the Bat." But not one in ten thousand could have named the man who wrote that poem.

His name was Ernest Lawrence Thayer, and he was born in Lawrence, Massachusetts, on August 14, 1863, one hundred years before the mighty Yankees made their celebrated strike-out. By the time he entered Harvard, the family had moved to Worcester, where Edward Davis Thayer, Ernest's well-to-do father, ran one of his several woolen mills. At Harvard, young Thayer made a brilliant record as a major in philosophy. William James was both his teacher and friend. Thayer wrote the annual Hasty Pudding play, and was editor of the Harvard *Lampoon,* the college's humor magazine. Samuel E. Winslow, captain of the senior baseball team (later he became a congressman from Massachusetts), was young Thayer's best friend. During his last year at Harvard, Thayer never missed a ball game.

Another friend of Thayer's college years was the *Lampoon*'s business manager, William Randolph Hearst. In 1885, when Thayer was graduated *magna cum laude*—he was Phi Beta Kappa and the Ivy orator of his class—Hearst was unceremoniously booted out of Harvard. (He had a habit of playing practical jokes that no one on the faculty thought funny, such as sending chamber pots to professors, their names inscribed thereon.) Hearst's father had recently bought the ailing San Francisco *Examiner* to promote his candidacy as United States senator from California. Now that young Will was in want of something to occupy his time, the elder Hearst turned the paper over to him.

Thayer, in the meantime, had settled in Paris to brush up on his French. Would he consider, Hearst cabled him, returning to the United States to write a humor column for the *Examiner*'s Sunday supplement? To the great annoyance of his father, who expected him to take over the American Woolen Mills some day, Thayer accepted Hearst's offer.

His contributions to the paper began in 1886. Most were unsigned, but starting in October, 1887, and continuing into December, he wrote a series of ballads that ran about every other week in the Sunday editions, under the by-line of "Phin." (At Harvard his friends had called him "Phinney.") Then ill health forced him to return to Worcester, but he continued for a while to send material to the *Examiner,* including one final ballad, "Casey at the Bat." It appeared on Sunday, June 3, 1888, sandwiched inconspicuously between editorials and a weekly column by Ambrose Bierce. Thayer was paid his usual fee for it—five dollars.

No one, including its author, paid much attention to "Casey." Baseball fans in San Francisco chuckled over it and a few eastern papers reprinted it, but it might have been quickly forgotten had it not been for a sequence of improbable events. In New York City a rising young comedian and singer, William DeWolf Hopper, was appearing in a comic opera called *Prince Methusalem.* One evening (the exact date is unknown; it was probably late in 1888 or early in 1889) the New York Giants and the Chicago White Stockings were invited to the show as guests of the management. What could he do on stage, Hopper wondered, for the special benefit of these men? A friend (and novelist), Archibald Clavering Gunter, said he had just the thing. He took from his pocket a ragged newspaper clipping that he had cut from the *Examiner* on a recent trip to San Francisco. It was "Casey."

Why not memorize the poem and deliver it on stage? Gunter suggested. Hopper did exactly that, in the middle of the second act, with the Giants in boxes on one side of the theatre and the White Stockings in boxes on the other. This is how Hopper recalled the scene in his memoirs, *Once a Clown, Always a Clown:*

When I dropped my voice to B flat, below low C, at "the multitude was awed," I remember seeing [the Giants' catcher] Buck Ewing's gallant mustachios give a single nervous twitch. And as the house, after a moment of startled silence, grasped the anticlimactic dénouement, it shouted its glee.

CASEY AT THE BAT*
A Ballad of the Republic, Sung in the Year 1888

*The outlook wasn't brilliant for the Mudville nine that day:
The score stood four to two with but one inning more to play.
And then when Cooney died at first, and Barrows did the same,
A sickly silence fell upon the patrons of the game.*

*A straggling few got up to go in deep despair. The rest
Clung to that hope which springs eternal in the human breast;
They thought if only Casey could but get a whack at that—
We'd put up even money now with Casey at the bat.*

*But Flynn preceded Casey, as did also Jimmy Blake,
And the former was a lulu and the latter was a cake;
So upon that stricken multitude grim melancholy sat,
For there seemed but little chance of Casey's getting to the bat.*

*But Flynn let drive a single, to the wonderment of all,
And Blake, the much despis-ed, tore the cover off the ball;
And when the dust had lifted, and the men saw what had occurred,
There was Johnnie safe at second and Flynn a-hugging third.*

*Then from 5,000 throats and more there rose a lusty yell;
It rumbled through the valley, it rattled in the dell;
It knocked upon the mountain and recoiled upon the flat,
For Casey, mighty Casey, was advancing to the bat.*

*There was ease in Casey's manner as he stepped into his place;
There was pride in Casey's bearing and a smile on Casey's face.
And when, responding to the cheers, he lightly doffed his hat,
No stranger in the crowd could doubt 'twas Casey at the bat.*

*As originally printed in the San Francisco Examiner on June 3, 1888

They had expected, as anyone does on hearing "Casey" for the first time, that the mighty batsman would slam the ball out of the lot, and a lesser bard would have had him do so, and thereby written merely a good sporting-page filler. The crowds do not flock into the American League parks when the Yankees play, solely in anticipation of seeing Babe Ruth whale the ball over the centerfield fence. That is a spectacle to be enjoyed even at the expense of the home team, but there always is a chance that the Babe will strike out, a sight even more healing to sore eyes, for the Sultan of Swat can miss the third strike just as furiously as he can meet it, and the contrast between the terrible threat of his swing and the futility of the result is a banquet for the malicious, which includes us all. There is no more completely satisfactory drama in literature than the fall of Humpty Dumpty.

Astonished and delighted with the way his audience responded to "Casey," Hopper made the recitation a permanent part of his repertoire. It became his most famous bit. Wherever he went, whatever the show in which he was appearing, there were always curtain shouts for "Casey." By his own count he recited it more than ten thousand times, experimenting with hundreds of slight variations in emphasis and gesture to keep his mind from wandering. It took him exactly five minutes and forty seconds to deliver the poem.

"When my name is called upon the resurrection morn," he related in his memoirs, "I shall, very probably ... arise, clear my throat and begin: 'The outlook wasn't brilliant for the Mudville nine that day.'" The poem, declared Hopper, is the only truly great comic poem written by an American. "It is as perfect an epitome of our national game today as it was when every player drank his coffee from a mustache cup. There are one or more Caseys in every league, bush or big, and there is no day in the playing season that this same supreme tragedy, as stark as Aristophanes for the moment, does not befall on some field."

By 1900 almost everyone in America had heard or read the poem, but almost no one knew who had written it. Hopper himself did not find out who the author was until about five years after he had begun reciting it. One evening, having delivered the poem in a Worcester theatre, he received a note inviting him to a local club to meet the author of "Casey." "Over the details of wassail that followed," Hopper wrote later, "I will draw a veil of charity." He did disclose, however, that the club members had persuaded Thayer himself to stand up and recite "Casey." Hopper declared it the worst delivery of the poem he had ever heard. "In a sweet, dulcet Harvard whisper he [Thayer] implored Casey to murder the umpire, and gave this cry of mass animal rage all the emphasis of a caterpillar wearing rubbers crawling on a velvet carpet."

From time to time various Caseys who actually played baseball in the late 1880's claimed to have been the inspiration for the ballad. But Thayer emphatically denied that he had had any specific ballplayer in mind for any of the men mentioned in "Casey." When the Syracuse *Post-Standard* wrote to ask him about this, he replied with a letter that is reprinted in full in Lee Allen's entertaining book on baseball, *The Hot Stove League:*

The verses owe their existence to my enthusiasm for college baseball, not as a player, but as a fan. . . . The poem has no basis in fact. The only Casey actually involved, I am sure about him, was not a ballplayer. He was a big, dour Irish lad of my high school days. While in high school, I composed and printed myself a very tiny sheet, less than two inches by three. In one issue, I ventured to gag, as we say, this Casey boy. He didn't like it and he told me so, and, as he discoursed, his big, clenched, red hands were white at the knuckles. This Casey's name never again appeared in the *Monohippic Gazette.* But I suspect the incident, many years after, suggested the title for the poem. It was a taunt thrown to the winds. God grant he never catches me.

Thayer remained in Worcester for many years, doing his best to please his father by managing one of the family mills. He kept quietly to himself, studying philosophy in spare hours and reading classical literature. He was a slightly built, soft-spoken man, inclined to deafness in his middle years, always gracious, charming, and modest. Although he dashed off four or five more comic ballads in 1896 for Hearst's New York *Journal,* he had a low opinion of his verse.

"During my brief connection with the *Examiner,*" Thayer once wrote, "I put out large quantities of nonsense, both prose and verse, sounding the whole newspaper gamut from advertisements to editorials. In general quality "Casey" (at least in my judgment) is neither better nor worse than much of the other stuff. Its persistent vogue is simply unaccountable, and it would be hard to say, all things considered, if it has given me more pleasure than annoyance. The constant wrangling about the authorship, from which I have tried to keep aloof, has certainly filled me with disgust." Throughout his life Thayer refused to discuss payments for reprintings of "Casey." "All I ask is never to be reminded of it again," he told one publisher.

Thayer retired to Santa Barbara, California, in 1912 and remained there until his death in 1940. Friends said that toward the end of his life he softened a bit in his scornful attitude toward "Casey." By then T. S. Eliot had written an admiring parody of the poem, and even professors of English, notably William Lyon Phelps of Yale, had hailed "Casey" as an

Ten thousand eyes were on him as he rubbed his hands with dirt;
Five thousand tongues applauded when he wiped them on his shirt.
Then while the writhing pitcher ground the ball into his hip,
Defiance gleamed in Casey's eye, a sneer curled Casey's lip.

And now the leather-covered sphere came hurtling through the air,
And Casey stood a-watching it in haughty grandeur there.
Close by the sturdy batsman the ball unheeded sped—
"That ain't my style," said Casey. "Strike one," the umpire said.

From the benches, black with people, there went up a muffled roar,
Like the beating of the storm-waves on a stern and distant shore.
"Kill him! Kill the umpire!" shouted some one on the stand;
And it's likely they'd have killed him had not Casey raised his hand.

With a smile of Christian charity great Casey's visage shone;
He stilled the rising tumult; he bade the game go on;
He signaled to the pitcher, and once more the spheroid flew;
But Casey still ignored it, and the umpire said, "Strike two."

"Fraud!" cried the maddened thousands, and echo answered fraud;
But one scornful look from Casey and the audience was awed.
They saw his face grow stern and cold, they saw his muscles strain,
And they knew that Casey wouldn't let that ball go by again.

The sneer is gone from Casey's lip, his teeth are clenched in hate;
He pounds with cruel violence his bat upon the plate.
And now the pitcher holds the ball, and now he lets it go,
And now the air is shattered by the force of Casey's blow.

Oh, somewhere in this favored land the sun is shining bright;
The band is playing somewhere, and somewhere hearts are light,
And somewhere men are laughing, and somewhere children shout;
But there is no joy in Mudville—mighty Casey has struck out.

Charles Dana Gibson depicted the mood of Mudville perfectly in these two drawings, called Two Strikes *and* Fanned Out.

now the president of New York City's Lincoln Center for the Performing Arts, wrote the music. Schuman is a baseball buff who, in his teens, seriously considered becoming a professional ballplayer. "Had I been a better catcher," he has written, "I might never have become a musician." Jeremy Gury, a writer, editor, and advertising agency executive, wrote the libretto. It is sad that Thayer did not live to see the opera. The details of its plot mesh so smoothly with the poem that one feels at once, "Yes, of course, that *must* have been the way it happened." *The Mighty Casey* has yet to have a full-scale production in New York City. (It is not easy to put on a short opera that calls for a forty-piece orchestra and a fifty-voice chorus!) After its Hartford premiere there was a television production of the opera in 1955, and it has been performed by small companies elsewhere.

How can one explain the undying popularity of Thayer's poem? Possibly because it is almost impossible to read it several times without memorizing whole chunks; there are lines expressed so perfectly, given the poem's intent, that one cannot imagine a word changed for the better. But perhaps the reason is because—with its careful build-up and its final fizzle—"Casey" is the incomparable, towering symbol of the great and glorious poop-out.

authentic native masterpiece. "The psychology of the hero and the psychology of the crowd leave nothing to be desired," Phelps wrote in *What I Like in Poetry*. "There is more knowledge of human nature displayed in this poem than in many of the works of the psychiatrist."

Since its first inauspicious appearance in 1888, "Casey" has constantly reappeared in new guises: once, in 1920, as a popular song; twice as a silent movie (the remake had Wallace Beery in the leading role); and twice more in Walt Disney cartoons. At least three recitations of "Casey" have been put on records —the first by Hopper himself in 1906, and the most recent, a children's record, by sportscaster Mel Allen. Several paperback editions of the poem have appeared, and finally in 1964 a handsome, illustrated hardcover version was published.

The most important elaboration of the Casey story is an opera, *The Mighty Casey*, which had its world premiere at Hartford, Connecticut, on May 4, 1953. William Schuman, a major American composer who is

Martin Gardner, who writes a column on mathematical games in the Scientific American, *has annotated several well-loved texts, most notably* Alice in Wonderland (The Annotated Alice). *His newest contribution is* The Annotated Casey At The Bat, *from which this article is taken. It will be published this autumn by Clarkson N. Potter.*

part of the ceremony, the musicians beat upon the sacks as instruments of music for their strange dances.

By the sides of these sacks, which they called *Eeh-tee-ka* (drums), there were two other articles of equal importance, which they called *Eeh-na-de* (rattles), made of dried undressed skins, shaped into the form of gourd-shells, which they also used, as will be seen, as another part of the music for their dances.

The sacks of water had the appearance of great antiquity, and the Mandans pretended that the water had been contained in them ever since the Deluge. At what time it had been originally put in, or when replenished, I consequently could not learn....

Such was the appearance of the interior of the Medicine Lodge during the three first (and part of the fourth) days. During the three first days, while things remained thus inside of the Medicine Lodge, there were many curious and grotesque amusements and ceremonies transpiring outside and around the "Big Canoe."

The principal of these, which they called *Bel-lohk-na-pick* (the bull dance), to the strict observance of which they attributed the coming of buffaloes to supply them with food, was one of an exceedingly grotesque and amusing character, and was danced four times on the first day, eight times on the second day, twelve times on the third day, and sixteen times on the fourth day, and always around the "Big Canoe," of which I have already spoken.

The chief actors in these strange scenes were eight men, with the entire skins of buffaloes thrown over them, enabling them closely to imitate the appearance and motions of those animals, as the bodies of the dancers were kept in a horizontal position, the horns and tails of the animals remaining on the skins, and the skins of the animals' heads served as masks, through the eyes of which the dancers were looking.

The eight men were all naked and painted exactly alike, and in the most extraordinary manner; their bodies, limbs, and faces being everywhere covered with black, red, or white paint. Each joint was marked with two white rings, one within the other, even to the joints in the under jaw, the fingers, and the toes; and the abdomens were painted to represent the face of an infant, the navel representing its mouth.

Each one of these characters also had a lock of buffalo's hair tied around the ankles, in his right hand a rattle (*she-shée-quoin*), and a slender staff six feet in length in the other; and carried on his back, above the buffalo skin, a bundle of willow-boughs, of the ordinary size of a bundle of wheat.

These eight men representing eight buffalo bulls, being divided into four pairs, took their positions on the four sides of the Ark, or "Big Canoe," representing thereby the four cardinal points; and between each couple of these, with his back turned to the "Big Canoe," was another figure engaged in the same dance, keeping step with the eight buffalo bulls, with a staff in one hand and a rattle in the other: and being four in number, answered again to the four cardinal points....

Two of these figures were painted jet black with charcoal and grease, whom they called *the night,* and the numerous white spots dotted over their bodies and limbs they called *stars*. The other two, who were painted from head to foot as red as vermilion could make them, with white stripes up and down over their bodies and limbs, were called the *morning rays* (symbols of day).

These twelve were the only figures actually engaged in the Bull *dance*, which was each time repeated in the same manner without any apparent variation. There were, however, a great number of characters, many of them representing various animals of the country, engaged in giving the whole effect to this strange scene, and all of which are worthy of a few remarks.

The bull dance was conducted by the old master of ceremonies (*O-kee-pa-ka-see-ka*) carrying his medicine pipe; his body entirely naked, and covered, as well as his hair, with yellow clay.

For each time that the bull dance was repeated, this man came out of the Medicine Lodge with the *medicine pipe* in his hands, bringing with him four old men carrying the tortoise drums, their bodies painted red, and headdresses of eagles' quills, and with them another old man with the two *she-shée-quoins* (rattles). These took their seats by the side of the "Big Canoe," and commenced drumming and rattling and singing, whilst the conductor of the ceremonies, with his medicine pipe in his hands, was leaning against the "Big Canoe" and crying in his full voice to the Great Spirit. Squatted on the ground, on the opposite side of the "Big Canoe," were two men with skins of grizzly bears thrown over them, using the skins as masks covering their faces. Their bodies were naked, and painted with yellow clay.

These characters, whom they called *grizzly bears,* were continually growling and threatening to devour everything before them, and interfering with the forms of the ceremony. To appease them and keep them quiet, the women were continually bringing and placing before them dishes of meat, which were as often snatched away and carried to the prairies by two men called *bald eagles,* whose bodies and limbs were painted black, whilst their heads and feet and hands

NEW-YORK HISTORICAL SOCIETY

On his journey to the upper Missouri in 1832, Catlin also visited the Sioux. He joined them in a buffalo hunt, concealed like his hosts in a wolf skin to avoid frightening the herd, but armed with sketchbook and pencil instead of bow and arrow.

were whitened with clay. These were again chased upon the prairies by a numerous group of small boys, whose bodies and limbs were painted yellow, and their heads white, wearing tails of white deer's hair, and whom they called *antelopes.*

Besides these there were two men representing *swans,* their bodies naked and painted white, and their noses and feet were painted black.

There were two men called *rattlesnakes,* their bodies naked and curiously painted, resembling that reptile; each holding a rattle in one hand and a bunch of wild sage in the other. There were two *beavers,* represented by two men entirely covered with dresses made of buffalo skins, except their heads, and wearing beavers' tails attached to their belts.

There were two men representing *vultures,* their bodies naked and painted brown, their heads and shoulders painted blue, and their noses red.

Two men represented *wolves,* their bodies naked, wearing wolfskins. These pursued the antelopes, and whenever they overtook one of them on the prairie, one or both of the grizzly bears came up and pretended to devour it, in revenge for the antelopes having devoured the meat given to the grizzly bears by the women.

All these characters closely imitated the habits of the animals they represented, and they all had some peculiar and appropriate songs, which they constantly chanted and sang during the dances, without even themselves (probably) knowing the meaning of them, they being strictly *medicine* songs, which are kept profound secrets from those of their own tribe, except those who have been regularly initiated into their *medicines* . . . at an early age, and at an exorbitant price; and I therefore failed to get a translation of them.

At the close of each of these bull dances, these representatives of animals and birds all set up the howl and growl peculiar to their species, in a deafening chorus; some dancing, some jumping, and others (apparently) flying; the *beavers* clapping with their tails, the *rattlesnakes* shaking their rattles, the *bears* striking with their paws, the *wolves* howling, and the buffaloes rolling in the sand or rearing upon their hind feet; and dancing off together to an adjoining lodge, where they remained in a curious and picturesque group until the master of ceremonies came again out of the Medicine Lodge, and leaning as before against the "Big Canoe," cried out for all the dancers, musicians, and the group of animals and birds to gather again around him. . . .

Of men performing their respective parts in the *bull dance,* representing the various animals, birds, and reptiles of the country, there were about forty, and forty boys representing antelopes—making a group in all of eighty figures, entirely naked, and painted from head to foot in the most fantastic shapes, and of all colours, as has been described; and the fifty young men resting in the Medicine Lodge, and waiting for the infliction of their tortures, were also naked and entirely covered with clay of various colours (as has been described), some red, some yellow, and others blue and green; so that of (probably) one hundred and thirty persons engaged in these picturesque scenes, *not one single inch of the natural colour of their bodies, their limbs, or their hair could be seen!*

During each and every one of these bull dances, the four old men who were beating on the sacks of water, were chanting forth their supplications to the Great Spirit for the continuation of his favours, in sending them buffaloes to supply them with food for the ensuing year. They were also exciting the courage and fortitude of the young men inside of the Medicine Lodge, who were listening to their prayers, by telling them that "the Great Spirit had opened his ears in their behalf; that the very atmosphere out-of-doors was full of peace and happiness for them when they got through; that the women and children could hold the mouths and paws of the grizzly bears; that they had invoked from day to day the Evil Spirit; that they were still challenging him to come, and yet he had not dared to make his appearance."

But, in the midst of the last dance on the fourth day, a sudden alarm throughout the group announced the arrival of a strange character from the West. Women were crying, dogs were howling, and all eyes were turned to the prairie, where, a mile or so in distance, was seen an individual man making his approach towards the village; his colour was black, and he was darting about in different directions, and in a zigzag course approached and entered the village, amidst the greatest (apparent) imaginable fear and consternation of the women and children.

This strange and frightful character, whom they called *O-ke-hée-de* (the owl or Evil Spirit), darted through the crowd where the buffalo dance was proceeding, alarming all he came in contact with. His body was painted jet black with pulverized charcoal and grease, with rings of white clay over his limbs and body. Indentations of white, like huge teeth, surrounded his mouth, and white rings surrounded his eyes. In his two hands he carried a sort of wand—a slender rod of eight feet in length, with a red ball at the end of it, which he slid about upon the ground as he ran.

On entering the crowd where the buffalo dance was going on, he directed his steps towards the groups of women, who retreated in the greatest alarm, tumbling over each other and screaming for help as he advanced upon them. At this moment of increased alarm the screams of the women had brought by his side *O-kee-pa-ka-see-ka* (the conductor of the ceremonies) with his medicine pipe, for their protection. This man had left the "Big Canoe," against which he was leaning and crying during the dance, and now thrust his *medicine* pipe before this hideous monster, and, looking him full in the eyes, held him motionless under its *charm,* until the women and children had withdrawn from his reach....

In several attempts of this kind the Evil Spirit was thus defeated, after which he came wandering back amongst the dancers, apparently much fatigued and disappointed; and the women gradually advancing and gathering around him, evidently less apprehensive of danger than a few moments before.

In this *distressing* dilemma he was approached by an old matron, who came up slyly behind him with both hands full of yellow dirt, which (by reaching around him) she suddenly dashed in his face, covering him from head to foot and changing his colour, as the dirt adhered to the undried bear's grease on his skin. As he turned around he received another handful, and another, from different quarters; and at length another snatched his wand from his hands, and broke it across her knee; others grasped the broken parts, and, snapping them into small bits, threw them into his face. His power was thus gone, and his colour changed: he began then to cry, and, bolting through the crowd, he made his way to the prairies, where he fell into the hands of a fresh swarm of women and girls (no doubt assembled there for the purpose) outside of the picket, who hailed him with screams and hisses and terms of reproach, whilst they were escorting him for a considerable distance over the prairie, and beating him with sticks and dirt.

He was at length seen escaping from this group of women, who were returning to the village, whilst he was disappearing over the plains . . . .

The crowd of women entered the village, and the area where the ceremony was transpiring, in triumph, and the fortunate one who had deprived him of his power was escorted by two matrons on each side. She was then lifted by her four female attendants on to the front of the Medicine Lodge, directly over its door, where she stood and harangued the multitude for some time; claiming that "she held the power of *creation,* and also the power of life and death over them; that she was the father of all the buffaloes, and that she could make them come or stay away, as she pleased."*

She then ordered the bull dance to be stopped—the four musicians to carry the four tortoise-drums into the Medicine Lodge. The assistant dancers, and all the other characters taking parts, were ordered into the dressing and painting lodge. The buffalo and human skulls on the floor of the Medicine Lodge she ordered to be hung on the four posts. She invited the chiefs to enter the Medicine Lodge, and (being seated) to witness the voluntary tortures of the young men, now to commence. . . .

* The publishing mores of Catlin's era would not permit a factual description of the procreative aspects of the bull dance or of the "power" captured from the Evil Spirit by his female pursuers, which was in reality a huge carved phallus. Hence, in the interests of complete accuracy, Catlin wrote a separate detailed account of the fertility rituals, which was inserted in the book as a detachable *Folium Reservatum.* "Scientific men," he explained, "who study not the *proprieties* of man, but Man, will receive this addendum in this form, and, I believe, duly appreciate and protect it."

Thus ended the bull dance (*bel-lohk-na-pick*) and other amusements at midday on the fourth day of the *O-kee-pa*, preparatory to the scenes of torture to take place in the Medicine Lodge; and the pleasing *moral* from these strange (and in some respects disgusting) modes, at once suggests itself, that in the midst of their religious ceremony the Evil Spirit had made his *entrée* for the purpose of doing mischief, and, having been defeated in all his designs by the magic power of the medicine pipe, on which all those ceremonies hung, he had been disarmed and driven out of the village in disgrace by the very part of the community he came to impose upon.

The *bull dance* and other grotesque scenes being finished outside of the Medicine Lodge, the torturing scene (or *pohk-hong* as they called it) commenced within, in the following manner.

The young men reclining around the sides of the Medicine Lodge, who had now reached the middle of the fourth day without eating, drinking, or sleeping, and consequently weakened and emaciated, commenced to submit to the operation of the knife and other instruments of torture.

Two men, who were to inflict the tortures, had taken their positions near the middle of the lodge; one, with a large knife with a sharp point and two edges, which were hacked with another knife in order to produce as much pain as possible, was ready to make the incisions through the flesh, and the other, prepared with a handful of splints of the size of a man's finger, and sharpened at both ends, to be passed through the wounds as soon as the knife was withdrawn.

The bodies of these two men, who were probably *medicine men,* were painted red, with their hands and feet black; and the one who made the incisions with the knife wore a mask, that the young men should

The Tragic Prescience of George Catlin

"Oh! how I love a people who don't live for the love of money," George Catlin once exclaimed. The artist never ceased to marvel at the guileless, trusting simplicity and unselfish generosity of his Indian hosts, who welcomed him without reservation into their homes, entertained him as best they could, and who, he explained, "are honest without laws, who have no jails and no poor-house."

This was hardly a popular point of view in the expansionist days of Catlin's America, and he was often accused, not without some validity, of romanticizing the Indian, both in his paintings and in his lucid writings. But at least part of Catlin's nostalgia sprang from his prophetic knowledge that the American Indian as he knew him could not survive in the white man's culture. Catlin wrote in 1835:

I have viewed man in the artless and innocent simplicity of nature, in the full enjoyment of the luxuries which God had bestowed upon him. I have seen him happier than kings or princes can be, with his pipe and little ones about him. I have seen him shrinking from civilized approach, which came with all its vices, like the dead of night upon him ... I have seen him shrinking from the soil and haunts of his boyhood, bursting the strongest ties which bound him to the earth and its pleasures; I have seen him set fire to his wigwam and smooth over the graves of his fathers ... [and] with tears of grief sliding over his cheeks, clap his hand in silence over his mouth, and take the last look over his fair hunting-grounds, and turn his face in sadness to the setting sun. All this I have seen performed in nature's silent dignity and grace ... and I have seen as often the approach of the bustling, busy, talking, whistling, hopping, elated, and exulting white man, with the first dip of the ploughshare, making sacrilegious trespass on the bones of the valiant dead. I have seen the skull, the pipe, and the tomahawk rise from the ground together in interrogations which the sophistry of the world can never answer. I have seen thus, in all its forms and features, the grand and irresistible march of civilization. I have seen this splendid juggernaut rolling on and beheld its sweeping desolation, and held converse with the happy thousands, living as yet beyond its influence, who have not been crushed, nor yet have dreamed of its approach.

I have stood amidst these unsophisticated people, and contemplated with feelings of deepest regret the certain approach of this overwhelming system, which will inevitably march on and prosper, until reluctant tears shall have watered every rod of this fair land; and from the towering cliffs of the Rocky Mountains, the luckless savage will turn back his swollen eye over the blue and illimitable hunting-grounds from whence he has fled, and there contemplate ... their splendid desolation....

All this is certain. Man's increase and the march of human improvements in this New World are as true and irresistible as the laws of nature, and he who could rise from his grave and speak, or would speak from the life some half century from this, would proclaim my prophecy true and fulfilled.

Catlin was off by only five years. On December 29, 1890, a unit of George Custer's old outfit, the 7th Cavalry, slaughtered with Hotchkiss guns some two hundred Sioux at Wounded Knee Creek in South Dakota. It was the last "battle" of the Indian wars.—*R. S. G.*

never know who gave them their wounds; and on their bodies and limbs they had conspicuously marked with paint the scars which they bore, as evidence that they had passed through the same ordeal.

To these two men one of the emaciated candidates at a time crawled up and submitted to the knife, which was passed under and through the integuments and flesh taken up between the thumb and forefinger of the operator, on each arm, above and below the elbow, over the *brachialis externus* and the *extensor radialis,* and on each leg above and below the knee, over the *vastus externus* and the *peroneus;* and also on each breast and each shoulder.

During this painful operation, most of these young men, as they took their position to be operated upon, observing me taking notes, beckoned me to look them in the face, and sat, without the apparent change of a muscle, smiling at me whilst the knife was passing through their flesh, the ripping sound of which, and the trickling of blood over their clay-covered bodies and limbs, filled my eyes with irresistible tears.

When these incisions were all made, and the splints passed through, a cord of raw hide was lowered down through the top of the wigwam, and fastened to the splints on the breasts or shoulders, by which the young man was to be raised up and suspended, by men placed on the top of the lodge for the purpose.

These cords having been attached to the splints on the breast or the shoulders, each one had his shield hung to some one of the splints: his *medicine bag* was held in his left hand, and a dried buffalo skull was attached to the splint on each lower leg and each lower arm, that its weight might prevent him from struggling; when, at a signal, by striking the cord, the men on top of the lodge commenced to draw him up. He was thus raised some three or four feet above the ground, until the buffalo heads and other articles attached to the wounds swung clear, when another man, his body red and his hands and feet black, stepped up, and, with a small pole, began to turn him around.

The turning was slow at first, and gradually increased until fainting ensued, when it ceased. In each case these young men submitted to the knife, to the insertion of the splints, and even to being hung and lifted up, without a perceptible murmur or a groan; but when the turning commenced, they began crying in the most heartrending tones to the Great Spirit, imploring him to enable them to bear and survive the painful ordeal they were entering on. This piteous prayer, the sounds of which no imagination can ever reach, and of which I could get no translation, seemed to be an established form, ejaculated alike by all, and continued until fainting commenced....

In each instance they were turned until they fainted and their cries were ended. Their heads hanging forwards and down, and their tongues distended, and becoming entirely motionless and silent, they had, in each instance, the appearance of a corpse....

When brought to this condition, without signs of animation, the lookers-on pronounced the word *dead! dead!* when the men who had turned them struck the cords with their poles, which was the signal for the men on top of the lodge to lower them to the ground, —the time of their suspension having been from fifteen to twenty minutes....

After this ordeal...a man advanced and withdrew the two splints by which they had been hung up, they having necessarily been passed under a portion of the *trapezius* or *pectoral* muscle, in order to support the weight of their bodies; but leaving all the others remaining in the flesh, to be got rid of in the manner yet to be described.

Each body lowered to the ground appeared like a loathsome and lifeless corpse. No one was allowed to offer them aid whilst they lay in this condition. They were here enjoying their inestimable privilege of voluntarily entrusting their lives to the keeping of the Great Spirit, and chose to remain there until the Great Spirit gave them strength to get up and walk away.

In each instance, as soon as they got strength enough *partly* to rise, and move their bodies to another part of the lodge, where there sat a man with a hatchet in his hand and a dried buffalo skull before him, his body red, his hands and feet black, and wearing a mask, they held up the little finger of the left hand towards the Great Spirit (offering it as a sacrifice, as they thanked him audibly, for having listened to their prayers and protected their lives in what they had just gone through), and laid it on the buffalo skull, where the man with the mask struck it off at a blow with the hatchet, close to the hand.

In several instances I saw them offer immediately after, and give, the *fore*finger of the same hand,— leaving only the two middle fingers and the thumb to hold the bow, the only weapon used in that hand. Instances had been known, and several such were subsequently shown to me amongst the chiefs and warriors, where they had given also the little finger of the *right* hand, a much greater sacrifice; and several famous men of the tribe were also shown to me, who proved, by the corresponding scars on their breasts and limbs, which they exhibited to me, that they had been several times, at their own option, through these horrid ordeals.

The young men seemed to take no care or notice of the wounds thus made, and neither bleeding nor inflammation to any extent ensued, though arteries were severed—owing probably to the checked circulation caused by the reduced state to which their four days and nights of fasting and other abstinence had brought them.

During the whole time of this cruel part of the ceremonies, the chiefs and other dignitaries of the tribe were looking on, to decide who amongst the young men were the hardiest and stoutest-hearted, who could hang the longest by his torn flesh without fainting, and who was soonest up after he had fainted—that they might decide whom to appoint to lead a war party, or to place at the most important posts, in time of war.

As soon as six or eight had passed through the ordeal as above described, they were led out of the Medicine Lodge, with the weights still hanging to their flesh and dragging on the ground, to undergo another and (perhaps) still more painful mode of suffering.

This part of the ceremony, which they called *Eeh-ke-náh-ka Na-pick* (the last race), took place in presence of the whole tribe, who were lookers-on. For this a circle was formed by the buffalo dancers (their masks thrown off) and others who had taken parts in the bull dance, now wearing headdresses of eagles' quills, and all connected by circular wreaths of willow-boughs held in their hands, who ran, with all possible speed and piercing yells, around the "Big Canoe"; and outside of that circle the bleeding young men thus led out, with all their buffalo skulls and other weights hanging to the splints, and dragging on the ground, were placed at equal distances, with two athletic young men assigned to each, one on each side, their bodies painted one half red and the other blue, and carrying

Superstition caused the Mandan squaws to object to having their husbands' portraits painted, but Catlin shamed the men into posing by telling them that white men never permitted their women to frighten them with "foolish whims."

a bunch of willow-boughs in one hand, who took them, by leather straps fastened to the wrists, and ran with them as fast as they could, around the "Big Canoe"; the buffalo skulls and other weights still dragging on the ground as they ran, amidst the deafening shouts of the bystanders and the runners in the inner circle, who raised their voices to the highest key, to drown the cries of the poor fellows thus suffering by the violence of their tortures.

The ambition of the young aspirants in this part of the ceremony was to decide who could run the longest under these circumstances without fainting, and who could be soonest on his feet again after having been brought to that extremity. So much were they exhausted, however, that the greater portion of them fainted and settled down before they had run half the circle, and were then violently dragged, even (in some cases) with their faces in the dirt, until every weight attached to their flesh was left behind.

This *must* be done to produce honourable scars, which could not be effected by withdrawing the splints endwise; the flesh must be *broken out,* leaving a scar an inch or more in length: and in order to do this, there were several instances where the buffalo skulls adhered so long that they were jumped upon by the bystanders as they were being dragged at full speed, which forced the splints out of the wounds by breaking the flesh, and the buffalo skulls were left behind.

The tortured youth, when thus freed from all weights, was left upon the ground, appearing like a mangled corpse, whilst his two torturers, having dropped their willow-boughs, were seen running through the crowd towards the prairies, as if to escape the punishment that would follow the commission of a heinous crime.

In this pitiable condition each sufferer was left, his life again entrusted to the keeping of the Great Spirit, the sacredness of which privilege no one had a right to infringe upon by offering a helping hand. Each one in turn lay in this condition until "the Great Spirit gave him strength to rise upon his feet," when he was seen, covered with marks of trickling blood, staggering through the crowd and entering his wigwam, where his wounds were probably dressed, and with food and sleep his strength was restored. . . . As soon as the six or eight thus treated were off from the ground, as many more were led out of the Medicine Lodge and passed through the same ordeal . . . and on the occasion I am describing, to the whole of which I was a spectator, I should think that about fifty suffered in succession, and in the same manner. . . .

It was natural for me to inquire, as I did, whether any of these young men ever died in the extreme part of this ceremony, and they could tell me of but one instance within their recollection, in which case the young man was left for three days upon the ground (unapproached by his relatives or by physicians) before they were quite certain that the Great Spirit did not intend to help him away. They all seemed to speak of this, however, as an enviable fate rather than as a misfortune; for "the Great Spirit had so willed it for some especial purpose, and no doubt for the young man's benefit."

After the Medicine Lodge had thus been cleared of its tortured inmates, the master or conductor of ceremonies returned to it alone, and, gathering up the edged tools which I have said were deposited there, and to be sacrificed to the water on the last day of the ceremony, he proceeded to the bank of the river, accompanied by all the tribe, in whose presence, and with much form and ceremony, he sacrificed them by throwing them into deep water from the rocks, from which they could never be recovered: and then announced that the Great Spirit must be thanked by all —and that the *O-kee-pa* was finished.

The end of the ceremony was, in a sense, the beginning of the controversy. For George Catlin had made two errors of fact which, though they do not seriously detract from the historical and ethnological value of his O-kee-pa, did provide Henry Rowe Schoolcraft with a factual basis to attack the artist's veracity. First, Catlin embraced the theory— later thoroughly discredited—that the Mandans were descendants of a Welsh expedition to the New World in the twelfth century. More seriously, Catlin published a second-hand report that the tribe had been totally annihilated by the smallpox epidemic of 1837. As Mr. Ewers points out in his fascinating introduction to the new edition of O-kee-pa, the Mandans were nearly wiped out by the epidemic Catlin heard about, but more than one hundred survived; they continued to perform the O-kee-pa until about 1890.

When the Coachman Was a Millionaire CONTINUED FROM PAGE 22

their clocks by the sound of the mail-coach horn, and the lore of stagecoaching was a tradition that became permanently imbedded in English literature.

In New York, soon after the Civil War, it became fashionable to drive four-in-hands to the races at Jerome Park or wherever one could see and be seen by the right people, and there were coaching clubs in the older cities along the Atlantic seaboard both before and after the formation of the Coaching Club. In time, even Brooklyn had a club which, typically enough, staged an annual carnival in Prospect Park. But these were all rather slapdash and informal and not at all what the gentlemen who formed the Coaching Club had in mind. Their objective was to establish standards of excellence in style and technique comparable to those they had observed abroad, and thus to encourage the development of coaching as a sport in America.

The element of sport in four-in-hand driving may seem remarkably obscure to the blasé possessors of automatic gearshifts and 300-horsepower engines. But managing four horses with the proper flourish and éclat required a skill and a degree of experience that made it quite satisfying in itself and that came to be widely recognized as an accomplishment of a high order. There was also the zest, particularly in England, of competing against the records established both by one's contemporaries and by professional coachmen in the days when the English mail coach was the fastest thing on wheels. For the driver and his passengers, the sense of speed, exhilaration, and freedom obtained on the top of a swaying, rattling road coach at twelve miles an hour far surpassed the confined and impersonal swiftness of trains. It is therefore not surprising that for many years coaching rivalled even fox hunting as the national pastime of England's upper classes. Although in this country it was more sedately conducted, it had a vast appeal for masculine tastes, if one had the time and the money to indulge in it.

To be eligible for membership in the Coaching Club a candidate had to be able to drive four horses and to own at least a quarter share of a drag. (A drag was virtually identical to a genuine road coach, though it was of somewhat lighter construction, and the two terms are used interchangeably here.) Voting was done by drags and there was no democratic nonsense about it. Four members who owned only one drag among them could be outvoted by two sole owners. Mere ownership of a drag and the ability to drive it, however, were far from being the only qualifications for membership. It was the unwritten and possibly unacknowledged qualifications that were the real test of eligibility. To the outsider it would appear that the great bond that knit Coaching Club men together was simply inherited wealth and the leisure it produced. But the true gentleman of leisure took such matters for granted; his explanation would have gone something like this: "The members of the Coaching Club are few in number and are bound together by unusual ties of close intimacy, loyal friendship, and harmony of tastes and mutual interest."

The years most fondly cherished in the memories of

old Coaching Club men were those from 1876 to 1884, when Madison Square was still the center of fashionable society in New York. It was in those years that the spring parades started and finished their triumphal prance up and down Fifth Avenue at the old Hotel Brunswick on the north side of the square at Twenty-sixth Street. Delmonico's restaurant was diagonally across Fifth Avenue, and other resorts of strictly masculine appeal were not far west on Twenty-fifth and Twenty-sixth streets. The residences of one's friends and relatives were all within pleasant walking distance, and the club itself was a permanent and honored guest of the exclusive Knickerbocker Club two blocks north on Twenty-eighth Street. The Brunswick, a bird-and-bottle paradise favored by visiting Britishers, was the rendezvous of the equine smart set. It was also the chief terminus of public-coaching routes. Stables lined Twenty-seventh Street between Fifth and Madison avenues behind the Brunswick, and the air was pungent with the aroma of the reign of the horse, still in its full glory. In such a harmonious setting the parades—with their long line of glistening coaches and drags, each graced with a proud coachman and the gay and elegant ladies and gentlemen who were his guests—were closer to jolly neighborhood parties than to the pomp-and-circumstance occasions they were later to become.

But the parades, for all their glittering display of social rank and eminence, were far from uppermost in the hearts of true coaching men as compared with the two other major activities of the club. One was the annual or semiannual trip to the country seats of hospitable members. The other was public coaching. The country trips, over roads still unmarred by the ravages of the automobile, were elegant adventures we can only envy today, and there is no difficulty in understanding their appeal. But at public coaching we must shake our heads in bewilderment, for here was a phenomenon so unique that it deserves a small but special niche in the history of American social customs.

Briefly, public coaching meant simply this: a gentleman or a group of gentlemen, of sufficient wealth and ample leisure, would undertake to drive a coach on a regular schedule over a specified route, carrying passengers who had paid a fare. Anyone, theoretically at least, could reserve a seat on such a coach, and by paying fifty cents or a dollar extra, he could ride on the box beside the coachman, who might be DeLancey Astor Kane or Reginald Rives or even, if he were very lucky, Alfred Gwynne Vanderbilt. It may be too much to expect to fathom why the Messrs. Kane, Rives, and Vanderbilt should have derived pleasure from such employment, but it is indisputable that they did. Were they, perhaps, classic examples of those punctilious gentlemen, blessed with the dignity and self-importance arising from the possession of wealth, whose conspicuous leisure was expressed in what Thorstein Veblen in *The Theory of the Leisure Class* termed "acts of substantial futility"? Perhaps. But no theory can account for the twinkle in Reg Rives's eyes as he posed for a picture, whip in hand and in full coaching regalia, nor even for his humble boast that "It was my good fortune, from the fact that I was not in business, to get a good deal more driving than my fellow committee men." And it certainly does not account for Alfred Vanderbilt's devotion to public coaching, which was unalloyed by any conceivable motives of social or pecuniary advantage. Mr. Vanderbilt was young and handsome, charming and unassuming, and yet he devoted a good part of his short life to driving coaches for hire. It may be wiser to accept such men and their zeal for public coaching in the simple terms they themselves would have used and understood.

In 1900, a year after Professor Veblen's now famous work appeared, Fairman Rogers, a member of the club since 1876, published *A Manual of Coaching*, the definitive work on the subject in America. Mr. Rogers' magnum opus, a labor of love brimming with erudite details painstakingly gathered over many years, would undoubtedly have been classified as a prime example of "substantial futility" by Professor Veblen. It is unlikely, however, that Mr. Rogers, or any of his fellow members for that matter, had ever heard of Professor Veblen; if they had, they would not have been impressed in the slightest. Writing in a bland, matter-of-fact style that somehow manages to convey an air of almost pontifical condescension, Mr. Rogers explained the lure of public coaching as a sport for gentlemen of his class:

Driving a coach on the road between fixed points, according to a regular time-table, with changes of horses, in imitation of old-fashioned business coaching, has a great fascination for the coaching man, and with good reason. It bears much the same relation to taking an afternoon drive at one's leisure that playing an instrument in an orchestra bears to practising solos at home. . . . A coachman never detects how little he knows until he undertakes to drive a fast road-coach. . . . In an afternoon drive in the park, if the reins are not quite right, if one horse pulls, if any one of many inaccuracies troubles the coachman, he can stop, try experiments, and re-arrange matters, and as he has no time to keep, he is not afraid of losing any; but on a fast road-coach it is very different; it is usually all that the teams can do to get over their ground in the time allotted; there is no opportunity to slow down in order to cool a fretful leader; if he will gallop, he has to gallop, or else to be handled with such skill as to bring him down to a trot without materially diminishing the pace; for minutes are precious.... Horses have to be shifted from one stage to another to make the best use of them or to counteract their peculiarities. Some horses go best in town, others in the country, a bad wheeler may make a good leader, changing sides may turn a troublesome horse into a good one, and all these matters are interesting and require judgment on the part of the coachman....

The driving itself, however, was only one of the joys of putting a coach on the road. As Reginald Rives pointed out, in a history of the club published in 1935, the fun commenced with the purchasing of the horses. The accepted rule, for a fast coach running out and back—or "down and up" in proper coaching usage—on the same day, was that there should be a horse to each mile of road. For a run of thirty miles, for instance, broken into six stages five miles apart, thirty horses would be required so as to have six teams plus one rest horse for each team. The economics

REUNION COACH,
"THE COMET."

Mr. *Korant*

Round Trip.

NEW YORK TO MORRIS PARK.

No. *1*

October *2nd* 1892.

peculiar to public coaching as a simulated commercial enterprise dictated the use of new horses each year and their sale, usually at a handsome profit, at the end of the season. The profit from the sale of these meticulously trained and matched animals was a matter of great pride, and on the rare occasions when the profit was sufficient so that a dividend could be declared on the whole operation, there was great rejoicing. Thus each February the gentlemen who planned to put a coach on the road during the coming season would brave the rigors of winter in Maine, where the proper type of horse was then to be obtained, to match wits with the horse dealers who lay eagerly in wait for them. Temperatures were chilly, but spirits were warm, and driving a hard bargain or even avoiding being fleeced too badly by the down-Easters produced a glow of achievement that may have been all the more satisfying because wealth made it so unnecessary.

The horses, once acquired, had to be trained and paired in teams. This took time and patience and skill, and although stable managers and grooms did the drudgery, their masters played an active role in the delicate task of blending the good and bad qualities of individual horses into well-matched teams for the road. While the horses were being trained, the stages for changing horses would be determined and stables at each stage would be engaged. Additional grooms might have to be hired to assist with the changes, and if they had had no previous experience in the intricacies of handling road horses so as to effect the change as swiftly as possible, the grooms too would have to be trained; a botched change could bring an otherwise excellent run to calamitous ruin. Then arrangements had to be made with the hotel chosen as the point of departure to handle the booking of seats; if the destination was a club, an agreement had to be reached extending guest privileges to the passengers for luncheon during the stopover. The latter made it imperative that the passengers should be presentable. Since fares were relatively modest and since, theoretically at least, anyone could book a seat, it seems to have been the duty of the booking clerks to discourage undesirable patrons. For the most part, the passengers were friends of the coachman or of other members of the club, or occasionally they were parvenus trying to become friends.

Mr. Rives, in his history at least, spoke disparagingly of only one of his passengers, to whom he referred as "a Mr. Y." Mr. Y had booked the entire coach for a party of his friends, but his booking had been disputed by Mr. X, who happened to be a friend of Mr. Rives. There was quite a contretemps in the lobby of the Holland House until Mr. Rives himself arrived on the scene, and, after weighing the claims of the disputants with judicial calm, reluctantly ruled in favor of Mr. Y. When the horn sounded the time of departure, however, and Mr. Y's party was safely ensconced on the coach, Mr. Y himself was still in the hotel making a phone call. Mr. Rives, naturally, pulled away on the dot, and poor Mr. Y was left fuming on the curb. He tried in vain to overtake the coach in a hansom cab, and then, by virtue of his authority as parks commissioner, ordered a mounted policeman to stop Mr. Rives. But the authority of being Reginald W. Rives, Esq., a member of the Coaching Club, took precedence over mere civic officialdom, and Rives refused to pull up until he had reached the first scheduled stop at the Fifty-ninth Street entrance to Central Park. As Mr. Y finally clambered aboard, trembling with rage and embarrassment, he shook a finger at Mr. Rives and said, "You wouldn't do that to one of your friends." "Please get up, and we will be off again," Mr. Rives replied rather curtly. He refrained from pointing out that one of *his* friends would have known better than to have expected such a departure from good form. It was a somber drive, and on the return trip Mr. Rives added a final touch to Mr. Y's humiliation by permitting a servant to ride in the place of honor on the box beside him.

The final fillip to the months of preparation, and the one stamping the whole endeavor with the seal of genuine entrepreneurship, came with the printing of a time-card showing the fares, the amount of baggage carried free, and the precise minute of arrival and departure at the stages and stopping points along the route. Invariably the time-card bore the stern admonition, "Passengers are cautioned to be on time." This was no idle gesture. "Making one's time" to the second was the special pride of public coachmen, and no delays were permitted nor any passenger waited for. Reginald Rives himself, in his history, boasted that "It is my record during the seven seasons in which I carried paid passengers over more than 10,000 miles on the road between the Holland House and the Ardsley Club that I had never been more than 45 seconds late at either end of the road."

Favorite runs were to the Westchester Country Club, then at Pelham, to the Getty House in Yonkers, and to the Ardsley Club at Ardsley, overlooking the Hudson. This last run, a distance of twenty-six miles, timed for two and a half hours each way with a three-hour stopover, was about the longest that could be done comfortably in one day, leaving ample time for conviviality and a leisurely luncheon before the trip back. The fare was $3 one way, $5 for the round trip —and the entire coach, seating twelve exclusive of the coachman and the guard, could be booked for $60. (The seats inside were not for sale. Though preferred by sensible folk in the days when stagecoaches were a necessity, the inside seats were now reserved for the road men who supervised the stages and for an occasional lady's maid.) There were longer runs made by going down one day and up the next. The longest regularly scheduled run ever made by public coach in America was one made in 1894 between the old Waldorf Hotel in New York and the Stratford in Philadelphia, a distance of over one hundred miles. Sponsored jointly by several members of the club and by a group of Philadelphians, it was also noteworthy as the only run in which double coaches—*i.e.*, coaches running in opposite directions on the same day—were used. It followed the route of old U.S. 1 and was a

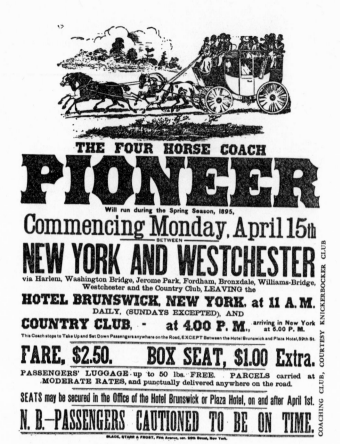

Frank Kintrea is a businessman from upstate New York who has an abiding interest in the foibles of the rich.

For further reading: The Coaching Club: Its History, Records & Activities, *by Reginald Rives (The Coaching Club, 1935);* A Manual of Coaching, *by Fairman Rogers (Lippincott, 1900).*

twelve-hour trip that included luncheon at the University Hotel in Princeton.

Although public coaching was the one true test of a coaching man's skill and devotion, the number of members who ever actually engaged in it was relatively small, and of these only a few persisted in it year after year. Of the 104 gentlemen who were members of the Coaching Club between 1876 and 1910, only twenty-five could qualify as members of this elite of the elite who took part in public coaching, and of these only six—Rives, Kane, Vanderbilt, Frederic Bronson, James Roosevelt Roosevelt, and George R. Read—put coaches on the road in three or more seasons.

Through the eighteen eighties and on into the early nineties, no club member could have dreamed that public coaching would not continue forever as a proper diversion for gentlemen. Not only did it have intrinsic merits as a sport, but, with its pseudo-commercial trappings, it provided an incomparable means of exhibiting one's disdain for the vulgarians who took money-making too seriously. In 1893, however, with the onset of a severe depression that lasted into 1897, the winds of change commenced to penetrate, if ever so slightly, even into the Coaching Club. Public coaching, of course, was essentially a social enterprise and was immune to the economic ills common to the nation as a whole. In fact, it had been blithely introduced in 1876 in the midst of one of the worst depressions the United States had ever known, and, as far as the mere financing was concerned, there was no reason for coaching to have been disturbed by the somewhat milder lapse in prosperity during the nineties. The years 1892, 1893, and 1894 had been banner years both for public coaching and for coaching in general, but as the depression dragged on, the temper of the times made coaching men wary of indulging in conspicuous displays of wealth and leisure, particularly as individuals.

Nevertheless, in spite of all adverse influences, the membership as a whole was strongly of the opinion that it was the duty of the club to carry on the traditions of public coaching. If the club itself should sponsor a run, it was believed that the onus of disapproval that might be incurred by individual proprietors would be avoided. Thus, in 1898, after two years in which no public coaches ran out of New York, the expense of putting the club's own *Pioneer* on the New York-to-Ardsley run was underwritten by a group of the members.

The *Pioneer*, laden with elegant ladies and gentlemen, was a great success at first. Its departures and arrivals at the Holland House on Fifth Avenue at Thirtieth Street were scenes of gaiety that stirred memories of the great days on Madison Square. It reached its peak in 1903, when a profit of $3,609.84 provided a festive occasion for the underwriters, but then came the sharp decline from 1904 to 1906, and the call for the special meeting on February 16, 1907.

When the meeting was called to order, the Committee on Public Coaching presented an "elaborate and exhaustive report," and a discussion ensued. The report made no definite recommendation, but it did recognize the fact that coaching faced ruthless competition from a new quarter. It was clear that the automobile, derided only a few years earlier as a fad, was here to stay. Its speed and power fulfilled one of man's age-old dreams, and the wondrous pride of ownership it inspired was irresistible. The production of autos had been rising fantastically, even during the prevailing depression: 4,192 had been produced in 1900, 33,500 in 1906, and there was no end in sight. No one could deny that the blasted things were becoming an infernal nuisance on the road, and it did no good to point out that the hard-surfacing of roads beyond city limits would inevitably bankrupt the nation. To some Coaching Club members it was unthinkable that a vehicle it had taken centuries to bring to the pinnacle of perfection—the English mail coach of the early nineteenth century—could so swiftly be replaced by a rickety, ugly, and still unreliable mechanical contraption. But the cold statistics were undeniable. Even Wall Street was beginning to show an interest in automobiles, and several club members sheepishly confessed taking a flyer in auto stocks themselves. Something should be done about it, but no one knew quite what, and the meeting came to a glum end with the decision not to place the *Pioneer* on the road during 1907. There were only scattered protests, but many members walked home shaking their heads in dismay.

After the club's withdrawal from public coaching, only young Alfred Vanderbilt had the courage to go it alone, and even he did not keep at it for more than a season longer. In the fall of 1907, he ran his coach *Venture* over the *Pioneer*'s old route between the Holland House and the Ardsley Club, and that was the end of genuine public coaching in this country.*

The last spring parade, a pale facsimile of its colorful predecessors, was held in 1910, and the last of the elegant trips to the country seat of a fellow member in the fall of 1916 was an ignoble anticlimax: the return trip was made by train. In the years before and after the First World War a few members maintained their rigs for junketing about the countryside in solitary splendor and for informal meets at Newport, but the war itself and the gaseous tyranny of the mass-produced automobile that followed ended forever any hope of a revival of coaching.

Although the sound of the horn and the jubilant cries of "tally-ho" were heard no more, the end of coaching was not to be the end of the Coaching Club. In 1925, the rules governing the eligibility of new members were amended to permit the admission of anyone "who shall exhibit to the officers of the Club satisfactory evidence that he participates actively in racing, hunting or the sport of polo." While the qualifications for becoming a member were thus broadened somewhat, the club itself has, if that is possible, steadily become more exclusive. Though the social limelight of the spring parades and of public coaching has faded, membership in the club now confers a quiet distinction that makes it a more coveted honor than ever.

The members still meet regularly three times a year at the Knickerbocker Club (now at Fifth Avenue and Sixty-second Street), and once each spring they turn out in a body for the annual running of the Coaching Club American Oaks, ordinarily held at Belmont Park. Horse-racing may be the sport of kings, but watching it is a far cry from the glories of driving a well-matched team on the open road.

* Mr. Vanderbilt ran public coaches on the famed Brighton Road in England from 1908 to 1914 and would undoubtedly have continued, but for the war. When he went down on the *Lusitania* in May, 1915, coaching lost a friend it could never replace.

READING, WRITING, AND HISTORY

By BRUCE CATTON

The Other Side Camp

One of the vainest of modern beliefs may be the assumption that it is civilization that makes life complicated. We like to dream that primitive man found existence very simple. He was at the mercy neither of his possessions, which were few, nor of his political and economic arrangements, which were extremely sketchy; all he had to do, apparently, was to solve the basic problems of survival—find shelter and food and some sort of security for life and limb—and he was home free. Life may have been hard, but it needed only to be lived, and while he was living it, primitive man did not need to think about it much.

As any ethnologist could testify, that is not quite the way it was. The simple savage did not have our worries, but he had plenty of his own, and a major concern of his life was the attempt to adjust himself to a universe that seemed just as complicated to him as ours does to us. For an illustration, read *Two Leggings: The Making of a Crow Warrior,* by Peter Nabokov.

Two Leggings was a war chief of the Crow nation, one of the most active and interesting of the Plains tribes. He was born sometime around 1840, and he died in the early 1920's, and a year or so before his life ended, his recollections were transcribed by William Wildschut, a field researcher for the Museum of the American Indian. A few years ago the manuscript came into the hands of Mr. Nabokov, a writer and a worker in the field of western Indian studies, who edited it and prepared it for publication. The book that now appears is the result, and it gives a revealing picture of the extraordinary amount of time and thought a savage warrior had to devote to the process of finding and maintaining his place in a baffling and unpredictable world.

Two Leggings was a hard-luck warrior. He spent nearly the first fifty years of his life fitting himself to understand and cope with the specialized society that lay between his horizons, and just as he had finished doing it, that society vanished forever. The life the Plains Indians led was over, every aspect of it gone beyond recall, and nothing the Indian had ever thought, done, or learned fitted him for the new existence the white man thrust upon him. Two Leggings wound up in a cabin on a reservation shortly before 1890, and there he spent his last thirty years. He dismissed those years, when he told his story to Mr. Wildschut, with these words: "Nothing happened after that. We just lived. There were no more war parties, no capturing of horses from the Piegans and the Sioux, no buffalo to hunt. There is nothing more to tell."

What makes the book interesting is its detailed picture of the kind of world Two Leggings lived in and the beliefs and actions it required of the people who lived in it. Like all of his fellows, Two Leggings was born to be a hunter and a warrior, and to win distinction, or indeed even to survive, he needed power and protection. He could get these only from the supernatural beings who inhabited the next world —the Without Fires people, who lived in the Other

Side Camp, and who laid down the rules and exerted the authority that controlled everything the Indian did. These Without Fires were divided into clans, just as Indian tribes were, and they included everything imaginable—sun and moon and stars, animals and birds, mountains and trees and flowers and rocks, plus the souls of the dead Indians that were visible on windy days in the little whirlwinds that dance over the plains.

To get power and protection, the Indian needed to be adopted by one or another of these supernaturals. Here the going began to be complicated, for some of these Without Fires were powerful chiefs, some of them were lesser chiefs, and some of them were not of much account. When you finally got a protector, it paid to get one of the good ones, because one in the lower ranks might not be able to take good care of you. In addition, the supernaturals were inveterate gamblers, and when they gambled they used their earthly children as stakes. Your protector in the Other Side Camp, be he ever so benign and active, might at any time lose you, through an unlucky throw of the bones, to some other supernatural. This, apparently, represented the Indian's recognition of a fact modern man also has to absorb: no matter how faithfully you follow the rules and conform to the proper pattern, a bit of bad luck can send it all down the drain at any moment.

In any case, it was above all things necessary for the Indian to get and to recognize a supernatural protector. He did this through dreams and visions, and to have these the young Indian had to go through a trying and painful ritual that might go on for years before it produced a satisfactory result. Once the proper dream had been dreamed it was of course necessary to have it interpreted, because to try to figure it out on your own hook was very risky, and here was where the medicine man came in. He would construe your dream for you, and tell you who or what your supernatural protector was, what other supernaturals were allied with him, and how you yourself had to order your life as a result. The medicine man was as devout a student of dreams as any Freudian analyst, and once he told you what your dream meant you could construct a proper medicine bundle which, if you used it right, would make you a great warrior and a successful hunter.

The medicine bundle was partly a religious symbol, partly an instrument of magic, and partly an earthly habitation for the Without Fires people who were represented in it. It could contain almost anything—a hawk's head, the skin of a fox, a couple of eagle's feathers, an oddly shaped rock, a bit of deerskin stitched with porcupine quills and wrapped around

an otter's skull—and it was treated with vast care and reverence because if you had no bundle you could not hope to accomplish anything.

Two Leggings set out to follow the ritual in his early teens, beginning by undergoing the agonizing self-torture of the sun dance. This was rough. The candidate let people thrust two wooden skewers through the fleshy part of his breast, watched as rawhide thongs were attached to each skewer and led to the top of a tall pole, and spent a day dancing about, leaning back against the strain of the instruments of pain and gazing steadfastly at the sun. Not everybody could stand it; Two Leggings remembered one young man who broke down in the middle of it, disengaged himself, and ran down to the river for water. Natu-

---

Two Leggings: The Making of a Crow Warrior, by Peter Nabokov, with a foreword by John C. Ewers. Thomas Y. Crowell Co., 226 pp. $6.95.

---

rally, he put a curse on the whole camp; the next war party was a flat failure, and it was all the fault of the man who could not quite stand the agony. (A description of a somewhat similar ceremony, among the Mandans, begins on page 30.)

Two Leggings stood it, and after the skewers had been torn out of him by the weight of his own body, he spent a couple of nights lying alone on a robe, looking up at the sky and waiting for whatever dream the combination of pain, weariness, and belief would bring him. Unfortunately, the dream he got was confused and inadequate, and as far as he could learn it conveyed no message. So a bit later he tried fasting on a mountain top.

This was not much better. He began by taking his knife and cutting off the tip of his left index finger; then he lay under the sky for three days and nights without food and drink, waiting for the supernaturals to speak to him. If they spoke at all, it was with blurred voices and confused meaning, and he was no better off than before. He tried it again, after a time, and then again, and although he no longer felt obliged to cut off a finger he cut gashes in his arms and waited for delirium and hunger to send him off to the Other Side Camp. He had certain dreams, but they were fuzzy. The supernaturals had been ignoring him.

It is interesting to note that at this point Two Leggings showed that he was as modern as any of us. He had had no worth-while dreams and he had not been able to get a medicine bundle, but he thought maybe he could cheat a little; that is, he set himself up in business as a youthful warrior leader and took a few small expeditions out against the nearest enemy tribes. As he ought to have known, these did not work out well. When he had successes they were small ones, and when he had failures they were bad. He was pressing his luck when his luck was bad, and as any present-day poker player could have told him, this is not the way to do it. Two Leggings at last gave up and threw himself on the mercy of the medicine men.

In short, he had to take a second best; he finally bought a medicine bundle from an elderly chief who, apparently, had had it and was ready to pass his power on to a deserving youth. As everybody knew, this was not nearly as good as getting your own bundle, but it could work; unable to get the power he needed by having and following his own visions, a man might get it by taking someone else's. In a manner of speaking, this worked. Two Leggings with his medicine bundle was at last able to lead war parties, and he became what his tribe called a pipeholder: which is to say that he was a war chief, carrying the sacred pipe that (along with all of the assorted bundles) somehow guided and directed the war party, and he won moderate distinction thereafter. He had by no means reached the top of the ladder. A pipeholder, as this book points out, was a sort of platoon lieutenant, not a top war chief. But since most actions in the Indian wars of the Old West were fought on the squad or platoon level, this was good enough. Two Leggings had at last made a success.

As is so often the case nowadays, there were built-in contradictions in the life of the Indian warrior. The man who died fighting was lucky. His Without Fires guardian immediately took him in charge, he became an honored warrior in the Other Side Camp, and his soul did not need to go whisking across the plain in a tiny dust cloud. To live to a ripe old age was much less honorable. Everybody wanted it, to be sure, and it showed that your sacred helper was a good gambler who never lost a game to a careless supernatural; besides, the Crow Indian enjoyed living as much as any man now enjoys it, and he knew that when at last he died he would have an honored place in the Other Side Camp. But the man who died in battle was the luckiest—except that this reflected on his supernatural helper, who could not have been very powerful if his earthly charge lost his life and his scalp. It also indicated that the young warrior in question

probably had not obeyed his otherworld father. As Two Leggings explained it:

When we receive a medicine our sacred helper gives us certain instructions. Sometimes we must not do certain things, like eating certain foods. If we disobey we may have bad luck or sickness or suffer a wound in battle. If we keep disobeying our sacred helper he will grow angry and place the life of his child as a stake against some powerful opponent who always wins. The souls of people who die this way are of a lower kind, but they are allowed to enter the Other Side Camp. However, the souls of suicides and murderers must roam the earth as ghosts.

Both ends, in short, worked against the middle, and even with the most steadfast faith and the most scrupulous care for observance of the proper ceremonies the Indian never quite knew where he was coming out. As we do today, he lived by prestige. If he could become a bureau chief, a branch manager, or a best-selling novelist—if, in other words, he could become a pipeholder—he had it made; except that to stand on the summit is to stand on a very slippery place. Even with the best medicine in the world, your war party could fail if your own skill and bravery were inadequate; on the other hand, the most brave and skillful man could fail if his medicine failed him. It was hard to figure.

The innocent and uncomplicated savage, thus, lived as we live, in a world he had never made. Life was infernally complicated and anything could happen. Man's biggest problem was to figure out the rules by which the world worked and then abide by them, and if things eventually went wrong it could only mean that the Without Fires party to whom he had entrusted his destiny had played a losing game with some other supernatural. Or, as a man might say nowadays, he was a good man who just did not get the breaks. The savage was singularly modern in his outlook. He just used a different language.

The point is that this particular Indian, Two Leggings, spent more than the first half of a long and active life trying to understand the complexities of the universe in which his lot had been cast, and at last he supposed that he had caught on. So he abided by the rules, made a substantial success, was entitled to call himself a sort of war chief—and then he found that the rules of the game had been changed while he was looking the other way. Then there was nothing left. As Two Leggings put it: "Nothing happened after that. . . . There is nothing more to tell."

Nothing more, except for the glimpse of a wild poetry by which these highly complicated men lived; the poetry, with its glimpse of the Other Side Camp and the Without Fires people, and the little puff-clouds of dancing dust shimmering across the endless plains.

We regret that in our June, 1967, issue the article "Down to the Sea," featuring the thirteen marine paintings by Edward Moran, did not give full credit to the United States Naval Academy Museum at Annapolis. We wish in particular to thank the curator, Captain Dale Mayberry, U.S.N. (Ret.), for making them available to us.

Death on the Range

CONTINUED FROM PAGE 48

Jackson rejected it and sought other paths. The paintings reproduced in AMERICAN HERITAGE are the result.

Jackson has always loved to draw. As a child in Chicago, where he was born in 1924, he spent hours sketching soldiers and animals, and while still in his teens he began to study painting at Chicago's Art Institute. But in 1938, at the age of fourteen, he did something dramatic, something perhaps as important for the future direction of his art as that later decision to abandon abstract painting: he ran away from home and became a ranch hand in Wyoming. After that the memories of the West—the vast open spaces, the cattle, and the loneliness of the cowboy—would always be vivid in his imagination. When Harry Jackson said later that he gave up abstraction because he felt that it was too limiting, that he wanted "to paint everything from satin to saddles," the saddles go back to those early days in Wyoming.

In 1942, after the United States had entered the Second World War, Jackson joined the Marines, and in the course of making reconnaissance sketches, was wounded on Tarawa and Saipan. Sent back to Los Angeles as an official Marine artist, he discovered modern art; and like most young American painters of the period, when the war ended he headed for New York to study. It was there during the next decade that his abstract paintings won him high recognition.

His dissatisfaction with the canvases he was producing is best explained by Jackson himself in an interview he gave in 1956, two years after he had quit the modernists: "I began to realize that there was more to art than just letting yourself go with paint. I felt like a traveller who had followed a road as far as it could take him in his direction. Now I was at the fork and had to let that road go on while I branched off my way." His decision to try to find another way of painting was greeted with dismay by friends. "You're on the wrong track, Harry; this is the most talented waste of time in America," one said. But in 1954 he sailed for Europe to study the old masters.

During the next few years, through studying in museums abroad and then returning to the United States to steep himself in such American artists as Remington, Homer, Eakins, Russell, and Hopper, Harry Jackson transformed himself into a traditional painter and sculptor. Today in his studios in Italy, Wyoming, and New York the products of his work come to life. The warning from his friend that "you're on the wrong track" has not been borne out, for not only has Jackson's own undoubted talent been recognized, but his shift from abstract to traditional art

came just before the wind of public interest began to shift in the same direction. Painting and sculpture based on western American themes, such as those that form an important part of Harry Jackson's work, have profited particularly by this shift. A Charles Russell painting, for example, recently brought $100,000, and a cast of Frederic Remington's *Bronco Buster*, which went for $1,100 in 1957, sold less than ten years later for $7,500. Jackson has had shows at important galleries and at major museums including the Amon Carter in Fort Worth and the Smithsonian Institution in Washington. But perhaps the finest recognition of all has come from a fellow western artist, Peter Hurd: "He is a man with a mission. Both as a painter and a sculptor he is equipped with the driving force and self-discipline so necessary to an artist. His mission is to communicate."

This desire to communicate is superbly illustrated by the two paintings on pages 48 and 49. The first to be completed was *The Range Burial*, a ten by twenty-one foot work commissioned in 1958 by the Coe Foundation of New York for the Whitney Gallery of Western Art in Cody, Wyoming. It represents six years of work: "I wanted to express," Jackson says, "how deep and authentic the respect for the dead can be on the part of ordinary men, with no trappings, and how nothing more than that is required. I was not interested in illustrating the specifics, so I didn't show the cuts and bruises on the dead man's body."

One of Jackson's many sketches for "The Range Burial." He also cast the scene in bronze as a preparation for the painting.

The second canvas, *The Stampede*, some nine and a half feet by almost twenty-one, was completed in 1960 and actually comes first in the story-telling sequence, for it shows how the dead man in the earlier picture was killed. "It was the overall pervading *state* I was trying to express," Jackson explains, "absolute chaos, hell-for-leather chaos. The death of the man was incidental—though not unimportant. Chaos, when all hell breaks loose—that was the important thing."

After seeing these two paintings, one understands fully what Peter Hurd meant when he called Jackson a man whose "mission is to communicate." Jackson himself has said that he wanted his paintings to "talk"; no one can doubt that in these two works he has given to canvas a tongue.   —*David G. Lowe*

The Aftermath of Treason CONTINUED FROM PAGE 17

June of 1778, following the evacuation of Philadelphia by a British army, Major General Benedict Arnold, then a widower of thirty-seven, entered the city in an appropriately elaborate procession to assume his new command as military governor. Few Philadelphians had ever before laid eyes on the famous "Hannibal of the Revolution." But few were ignorant of his contributions to the American cause—of his bravery on the battlefields of Quebec and Danbury and Bemis Heights. From the open carriage bearing him up Walnut Street he acknowledged the cheers of the crowd with blunt nods of his big head, his twice-wounded left leg resting on a pillow, his blue eyes startlingly pale in a swarthy, thrusting, truculently handsome face.

It is doubtful that Peggy Shippen was on hand, more likely that she was behind the doors of her family's tall brick house on fashionable South Fourth Street. Although he regarded himself as a neutralist, her father, Judge Edward Shippen, was a Loyalist in the eyes of the Pennsylvania authorities. She was the youngest of his five children, a willowy creature with a small, spoiled, eager mouth, fetchingly plump cheeks, and wide, solemn eyes somewhere between hazel and gray. She had enjoyed the British occupation. For nine dizzying months life had been a round of hops and routs, of candlelit suppers and evenings at the theatre, of gorgeously accoutered young officers coming to pay their respects.

We do not know when or where she and Arnold met; possibly it was at one of the parties the commandant of Philadelphia gave at his elegant headquarters on Market Street. We do know that in spite of the nineteen years' difference in their ages the attraction was mutual. Benedict Arnold saw in Peggy Shippen the same desire for the good things of this world that burned at the core of his own restless being. She in turn sensed in the ruthless force that seemed to emanate from him the promise of a glittering fulfillment. They were married on April 8, 1779. Before the honeymoon was over, Arnold had offered his services to Sir Henry Clinton, the British commander in chief in America, thus initiating the conspiracy that a year and a half later would take him and Peggy to West Point and catastrophe.

It is clear from Sir Henry Clinton's papers, opened to scholars some forty years ago, that Peggy was aware of her husband's treasonous negotiations from the beginning and to some extent was involved in them. Only hearsay supports the story of her confession to an acquaintance that it was she who had persuaded

her husband to betray his country, but such an action would have been in keeping with her character and background. Unlike her moderate father, Peggy was an ardent Tory, and she was ambitious. She realized that if the General aided the British substantially, he would be well rewarded. A grateful king might even give him a title. Then some day, after years of gracious living in England, she could return to Philadelphia to be deferred to by her friends as "Lady Arnold."

It was the collapse of these dreams that sent her into apparent hysterics on September 25, 1780, when word reached West Point that the treason conspiracy had been discovered, and her frantic husband made his last-minute escape, leaving Peggy and her six-month-old son to the kind mercies of George Washington and his aides. Washington gave her a choice. She could join her husband in British-held New York or her family in Philadelphia. She chose Philadelphia, but the local authorities refused to let her stay. By November she and her baby were in New York, living with Arnold in a fine house he had leased next door to British headquarters at Broadway and Wall Street.

No blaring trumpets had welcomed the fleeing traitor to Great Britain's American stronghold. Not that he had cause to complain. Sir Henry Clinton and his generals punctiliously bestowed on him all the consideration due a competent military man who in their opinion, of course, was merely a rebel who had seen the light and had returned to his proper allegiance. Treason had deprived Arnold of his American rank of major general; but Sir Henry assigned to him the highest British military rating ever given an American colonial, that of colonel of a regiment, with the rank of brigadier general of provincials and the authority to raise a Loyalist legion.

Below the upper echelons at headquarters, however, Arnold's presence was resented. A local newspaper noted that the "General . . . is a very unpopular character in the British army, nor can all the patronage he meets with from the commander-in-chief procure him respectability." To a man, the English subalterns refused to join his unit, the American Legion Refugees. He was compelled to officer it from the Loyal American Corps, commanded by the elderly New York Tory Colonel Beverly Robinson. His efforts to fill the ranks were time-consuming and only partly successful. Even after his Legion had achieved respectable proportions, Sir Henry Clinton showed great reluctance in making use of it. The cautious English commander was aware that beyond the ramparts of New York the traitor would be the object of fierce

84

enemy action. Even within the city Arnold was unsafe: an elaborate scheme by the Americans to kidnap him from the garden of his home one evening came within a hairbreadth of succeeding.

Only twice did Sir Henry permit the traitor to take to the field against his countrymen. Both were diversionary forays of no strategic importance. The first took Arnold to the James River in Virginia, where, in response to Governor Thomas Jefferson's refusal to turn over the tobacco stores at Richmond, he ordered his soldiers to burn the warehouses and gave them carte blanche to plunder the city. His second expedition took him to New London and Groton, Connecticut, only a few miles down the Thames River from his native Norwich. There his reduction of two small American forts ended in scenes of horror as his rampaging soldiers—contrary to Arnold's intentions, according to Sir Henry Clinton—massacred the garrison of one of the surrendered forts, murdered its commandant in cold blood, and set fire to New London.

Of Peggy's life in Manhattan we catch only infrequent glimpses, most of them from Mrs. Samuel Shoemaker, a Philadelphia Loyalist who had come north to be with her husband. "P[eggy] A," Mrs. Shoemaker was writing her daughter in Philadelphia in November of 1780, "is not so much admired here for her Beauty as one might have expected. All allow she has great Sweetness in her Countenance, but wants Animation"—a statement which suggests that the young wife was still profoundly shaken by the miscarriage of her husband's treason and the blow to her once high hopes. In a later letter Mrs. Shoemaker announced that at a headquarters ball Peggy had "appeared a star of the first magnitude, and had every attention paid her as if she had been Lady Clinton. Is not this fine encouragement for generals to follow A[rnold]'s example?"

On December 15, 1781, the Arnolds sailed for England. Peggy and her children, including a second son born in Manhattan, took passage on a private vessel. Arnold travelled on the warship *Robuste,* where one of his companions was his good friend Charles, Earl Cornwallis, free on parole following the defeat of his army at Yorktown.

Halfway across the Atlantic, a storm struck the 150-ship fleet to which both vessels were attached. The *Robuste* (despite her name) sprang a leak. Arnold moved to the transport *Edward;* Peggy's ship wallowed through. On Tuesday, January 22, 1782, according to next day's London *Daily Advertiser,* both of the Arnolds "arrived in the Metropolis." Typical English weather greeted them: a brisk wind and a "small rain" that drenched the winding streets, the wooded parks, and the 750,000 inhabitants of busy, mellow, dirty eighteenth-century London.

The political winds were just as brisk. Since Yorktown, the leaders of the out-of-government party in England had been clamoring for an end to the "American war." King George III and his government insisted that it go on. Sir Henry Clinton had given Arnold a letter of introduction to Lord George Germain, Secretary of State for the Colonies, who treated him with respect.

For a few weeks Arnold's name figured prominently in the local press. He attended court at St. James's Palace. Sir Walter Stirling, a London banker and a relative of Mrs. Arnold's, introduced him to the king, and reporters spotted him strolling in the public gardens in intimate conversation with his Majesty and the Prince of Wales. From Paris, Benjamin Franklin wrote to America that "we hear much of audiences given to Arnold, and his being present at councils." On the fourth of February the *Daily Advertiser* announced that Arnold was "shortly to return back to America, and to have the command of the Loyalists, a Prosecution of the War having been determined upon." This report was singularly inaccurate, since the day was near when Parliament would compel King George to make peace with his "revolted colonies" and recognize their independence.

Peggy was not slighted. On Monday, February 10, Lady Amherst presented her at court: the king pronounced her "the most beautiful woman he had ever seen," and the queen instructed her ladies "to pay much attention to her."

But if a mild warmth suffused the reception of the Arnolds in some quarters, something closer to contempt was apparent in others. The March issue of

The Arnolds' marriage began in the Shippen house in Philadelphia, where the wedding took place in 1779; it endured, through many vicissitudes, until Arnold's death in 1801.

85

London's widely-read *Gentleman's Magazine* quoted a peer of the realm who complained bitterly about "placing at the King's elbow a man perhaps the most obnoxious to the feelings of the Americans of any in the King's dominions at the moment the House was addressing his Majesty to put an end to the American war." In the Commons, Edmund Burke expressed the hope that the government would not put the traitor "at the head of a part of a British army" lest "the sentiments of true honor, which every British officer [holds] dearer than life, should be afflicted."

Burke need not have worried. With the fall of the war ministry in March of 1782, what little prestige Arnold had enjoyed in London came to an end. He remained a general, which is to say he was so addressed; but England gave him no military post and his anxious and frequently repeated efforts to obtain one were fruitless. In 1784, restless and without occupation, he applied for a position with the East India Company. The answer to his application, written by George Johnstone, a director of the company, was a masterpiece of icy English honesty. The gist of it was that even successful traitors are "seldom greatly loved" by their beneficiaries. As a traitor who had failed, Arnold could never hope for employment with the powerful East India Company.

The Arnolds' first home in London was on Portman Square. During the years to come they would occupy a succession of leased houses in this new and moderately fashionable neighborhood, a short distance northeast of what is now Marble Arch at the juncture of Oxford Street and Park Lane. Several American Loyalists lived in the area. Peggy established a lasting friendship with Ann and Sarah Fitch and their brother William, members of a once well known New England family. She visited regularly at the Fitches' country home in Essex and frequently accompanied them to Bath and other watering spots.

As Arnold receded from prominence, so did Peggy, although in her case the shift was more a matter of choice than of necessity. As late as 1785 she was still highly esteemed in London. A visiting Philadelphian informed his wife that Mrs. Arnold "is an amiable lady, and was her husband dead would be much noticed." According to her sympathetic but conscientious biographer and descendant, Lewis Burd Walker, however, Peggy made little or no effort to capitalize on her personal popularity. "We have no account," Walker writes, "of her being present at any scene of gayety and pleasure." Shock and suffering had left their mark. Those who had known the party-loving belle of Revolutionary Philadelphia would scarcely have recognized the devoted wife and mother of Portman Square. Repeatedly in her letters home she spoke

George III received Arnold with respect, but not all his nobles followed suit. At the palace one evening, the Earl of Balcarres (center), who had opposed Arnold at Saratoga, snubbed him, reportedly saying: "I honored you as a brave man in battle; I despise you as a traitor to your country..."

Harper's New Monthly Magazine, NOVEMBER, 1861

of her "struggle to keep up an appearance" for the sake of her "children's rising prospects."

At the time of her arrival in England her American-born sons, Edward and James, were both under two years old. A boy and a girl, born in 1783 and 1784, died in infancy, but 1785 saw the birth of a daughter, Sophia, who though often ill lived to become a dear companion to her mother. Later came two more sons: George, born in 1787; and William, who, arriving in 1798, long after the others, was spoken of as Little William. Arnold already had three sons by his first wife, Benedict, Richard, and Henry, all of whom had remained in the United States. It tells us much about Peggy that she gave thoughtful love and attention to her stepsons. When, in his twenty-fourth year, Richard wrote that he had fallen in love, Peggy did not hesitate to express the hope, in a long, warm letter, that he would refrain from marrying the young woman "till you are enabled to support her in a comfortable style."

She was unfailingly kind to the traitor's only surviving sister, who had taken over the care of the three eldest sons after the death of their mother in 1775. Hannah Arnold openly resented her brother's second marriage. She once wrote him a spinsterish letter, accusing his young wife of "frequent assignations" with "a certain chancellor," meaning Robert R. Livingston of New York. The General displayed no jealousy, presumably because none was justified.

No straying from matrimonial rectitude can be attributed to Peggy Arnold, whose letters reveal a strong religious bent, strangely Calvinistic for a woman brought up in the relative leniency of the Church of England. "These things," she once observed of a shower of personal misfortunes, "are wisely ordained by the Almighty for some good purpose, and His justice and mercy we cannot doubt."

In the early years of their exile the Arnolds were free of financial worry. Arnold's "rewards" for treason were substantial. During the long negotiations with the British prior to his attempt to betray West Point, he had demanded £20,000 if he succeeded, £10,000 if he did not. Sir Henry Clinton agreed to the £20,000 for success, but would go no higher than £6,000 for failure. On October 18, 1780, only a few weeks after the collapse of the conspiracy, Arnold was paid this amount plus £315 for "expenses." These sums were but the beginning. Although in 1780 Benedict, Jr., the eldest of the traitor's sons by his earlier marriage, was only twelve, he was given a commission in the British Army carrying half pay for life; and in 1781 his younger brothers were commissioned on the same terms. Arnold himself, during his active service in the British Army, received a provincial brigadier's pay, £650 a year. When the treaty of peace was signed in 1783, this fell to £225, the half pay of a cavalry colonel. The traitor also profited handsomely from his marauding expedition to Virginia, which seized American shipping on the James. Arnold's share of the prize money appears to have been in excess of £2,000.

Shortly before the general left New York he dispatched £5,000 of his capital to London, where his broker then converted it into £7,000 worth of four per cent consolidated annuities. Subsequent to the Arnolds' arrival in the British capital, the king added to their fortunes. On March 17, 1782, George informed his paymaster that it "is Our will and pleasure . . . that an annuity or yearly pension of five hundred pounds be . . . paid . . . unto Mrs. Arnold, wife of our trusty and well beloved Brigadier General Benedict Arnold. . . ." At about the same time, the British government provided for Peggy's children, including those yet unborn, each of them getting a pension of eighty pounds net per year. Historians differ as to what dollar value can be placed on Arnold's compensations for treason. One puts it as high as $120,000 in modern purchasing power; another as low as $55,000. Whatever the proper figure, the Arnolds could have lived on their income comfortably, indeed "genteelly," for an indefinite period had the General been content. But to say that Benedict Arnold was never content is to epitomize his life.

In 1785 he submitted to the Commissioners on Loyalist Claims a "memorial" requesting £16,125 over and above the monies he had already received. He described this additional sum as a "moderate computation" of the losses he had incurred by coming over to the British.

One of his claims dealt with Mount Pleasant, the baronial country seat near Philadelphia that he had purchased in the spring of 1779 as a wedding present for Peggy. After exposure of his treason, the Pennsylvania authorities confiscated Mount Pleasant. Arnold said it was worth £5,000—£1,000 above a contemporary American appraisal; he did not add that his father-in-law had purchased the property from the Pennsylvania authorities and was holding it for his daughter. Another of Arnold's claims was even emptier. Writing in the third person, he told the British commissioners that "in consequence of his loyalty and engagements with Sir Henry Clinton he [had] refused the command of the American Army in South Carolina, offered him . . . by Washington, which was afterwards given to [Major General Nathanael] Greene, who (the memorialist is informed) has been rewarded by the states of the Carolinas and Virginia with the sum of £20,000 sterling for his services, which would probably have been given to the memorialist had he accepted the command." As a matter of fact Washington had never offered the South Carolina command to Arnold. Perhaps the hollow foundation of these claims eventually bothered the traitor himself. On April 26, 1786, he withdrew his memorial to the commissioners, explaining in a letter inscribed on gilt-edged paper that Clinton had compensated him for his losses, and that his wife had received her pension.

Prior to the Revolution Arnold had prospered as a maritime merchant, working out of New Haven, Connecticut, and sailing his own ships up and down the American coast, buying, selling—and smuggling—livestock and provisions. In 1785 he purchased a brig, moved Peggy and the children to a smaller house in the Portman Square area, and left England for the largely Loyalist-built seaport of St. John, on the Bay of Fundy, in the Canadian province of New Brunswick. En route he put in at Halifax, greatly surprising the inhabitants there. "Will you believe General Arnold is here . . . ?" one wrote to a friend in St. John. "He is bound for your city, which he will of course prefer to Halifax, and settle with you. Give you joy of the acquisition."

In St. John, Arnold purchased property and started a merchandising enterprise in partnership with an American Loyalist. It was during his first winter in St. John that he became the father of an illegitimate son, John Sage, later mentioned in his will. The name of John's mother remains a secret of history—

and possibly of Peggy, to whom, according to Willard M. Wallace, one of Arnold's best biographers, he confessed all and was forgiven, when in 1787 he returned to England long enough to place their younger sons with a private family and to move Peggy and their infant daughter to New Brunswick.

Back in St. John in July of that year, he bought a house big enough to accommodate his sister Hannah and the three sons of his former marriage, who came up from New England. Simultaneously he expanded his business, setting up trading stations on Campobello Island and at Fredericton, the wilderness-rimmed capital of the province.

Once on North American soil, Peggy began making preparations to visit her family in Philadelphia. Twice she had to defer the trip, first because of the birth of another child, then because Arnold was away on a long trading journey. Most of 1789 had passed before she boarded a packet for the States, carrying baby George in her arms and accompanied by a maid.

At home she was relieved to find her mother in good spirits in spite of a crippling illness. Her father too appeared to be content and happy in a new and elevated position. After the war, Philadelphians had found it easy to forgive capable, clear-thinking Judge Edward Shippen for his Loyalist sympathies and to to make use of his talents. He was now on the state's highest bench. A decade hence he would become chief justice of Pennsylvania, the title by which posterity remembers him. Before Arnold entered her life, Peggy had centered her affections on the Judge, and unquestionably it was a pleasure for her to be with him again. She could also chat for hours with her eldest and favorite sister, Elizabeth. Her brother Edward and her sisters had married, so there were nephews and nieces to be met and fondled. Still, her visit was hardly the triumphant return to the home town that Peggy had conjured up in her lively mind.

Snobbish Philadelphians disapproved of her frequent references to "his Majesty." Old friends, even some relatives, snubbed her on the streets. Knots of people gathered in front of her father's house to stare coldly as the "traitor's wife" came and went. "How difficult it is," she wrote sister Betsy in the summer of 1790, a few weeks after her return to St. John, "to know what will contribute to our happiness in this life. I had hoped that by paying my beloved friends a last visit, I should insure to myself some portion of it, but I find it far otherwise."

Peggy wrote that it was cold in New Brunswick that summer. Gloomy fogs were rolling in from the sea and an epidemic of influenza was raging. She could have mentioned other troubles. Her husband was widely disliked. When, shortly before Peggy's trip south, the traitor's waterfront warehouse burned to the ground, gossiping tongues said he had set the fire to collect the insurance, although one of his older sons was asleep in the building at the time and barely escaped with his life, and Arnold himself was thousands of miles away on a trading jaunt. Subsequently he and his partner, Munson Hayt, parted company under unpleasant circumstances. Hayt said the General and his wife had cheated him of £700. In a legal plea he admitted proclaiming "with a loud voice" that Arnold had burned his own warehouse. He contended it was not in his power to blacken Arnold's character because it was already "as black as it can be." The General countered with a suit for slander. He won, but the judge, a Loyalist from New Jersey, awarded him only two shillings and sixpence instead of the £5,000 damages he had asked.

During the Arnolds' last year in St. John, 1791, the long-standing dislike of the General assumed violent form. In the spring a mob overran the front lawn of his home. The angrily shouting citizens were burning an effigy labeled "traitor" when the troops arrived to disperse them. A few weeks later the Arnolds signalled their imminent departure for England with an advertisement in the *Royal Gazette* offering their New Brunswick properties for sale. The household items listed in the newspaper included "a set of elegant cabriole chairs covered with blue damask, sopha to correspond," a "desert set of Wedgewood Gilt Ware," "a Terrestrial Globe," and "a Lady's elegant Saddle and Bridle." They sailed on New Year's day. On the following February 26 Arnold wrote his agent in St. John, Jonathan Bliss, that their reception in London had "been very pleasant . . . and I cannot help viewing your great city as a shipwreck from which I have escaped."

Actually little in the way of better fortune awaited him in England. In the spring of 1792 the Earl of Lauderdale made a slighting remark about him in the House of Lords. Arnold challenged, and on June 26 Peggy wrote her father to ignore a "paragraph" in the "public Papers of a few days back . . . mentioning that Genl. A is killed in a Duel with the Earl of Lauderdale. This was for some time so generally believed, that our friends were flocking to the house, to condole. . . ." In fact, Peggy revealed, the duel was still in the offing and her "situation" remained "a very unhappy one, till the Affair is settled; but I call all my fortitude to my aid, to prevent my sinking under it, which would unman him [Arnold] and prevent his acting himself—I am perfectly silent on the subject; for weak Woman as I am, I would not wish to prevent what would be deemed necessary to preserve his honor."

Fortunately, on July 6 Peggy could write her father that the duel had come and gone with nobody the worse. "The time appointed," she reported, "was seven o'clock on Sunday morning last—Mr. Charles Fox, as second to Lord Lauderdale; Lord Hawke, the General's. It was agreed that they should fire at the same time, upon a word given, which the General did without effect." Then Lord Lauderdale "refused to fire," and after a short parley apologized to Arnold's satisfaction. Peggy added that it "has been highly gratifying to find the General's conduct so much applauded."

Encouraged by the favorable publicity arising from his encounter with Lauderdale, Arnold renewed his pleas for a government post, preferably military. A recommendation from Sir Henry Clinton, a string of letters from Arnold—nothing availed, and in 1794 he returned to his old trade on the high seas.

England and France were at war. French privateers

One of the few occasions on which Arnold was permitted to lead troops against his former comrades was on a raid in Connecticut in 1781. Here Arnold watches in displeasure as his men, contrary to his orders, set fire to New London.

were roaming the English Channel. While Arnold was waiting to embark in Falmouth, a storm-beaten ship heading for America came in to port. Among its passengers was Charles Maurice de Talleyrand-Périgord, later to win fame as Napoleon's foreign minister, then a refugee from the Jacobin rulers of republican France. That night Talleyrand had an experience worth noting: it records Arnold's only known mention in conversation, following his departure from America, of the country he had betrayed. Talleyrand wrote in his memoirs:

The innkeeper at whose place I had my meals informed me that one of his lodgers was an American general. Thereupon I expressed the desire of seeing that gentleman, and, shortly after, I was introduced to him. After the usual exchange of greetings . . . I ventured to request from him some letters of introduction to his friends in America.

"No," he replied, and after a few moments of silence, noticing my surprise, he added, "I am perhaps the only American who cannot give you letters for his own country . . . all the relations I had there are now broken . . . I must never return to the States."

He dared not tell me his name. It was General Arnold. I must confess that I felt much pity for him, for which political puritans will perhaps blame me, but with which I do not reproach myself, for I witnessed his agony.

Late June of 1794 found Arnold approaching Pointe-à-Pitre on the Guadeloupe island of Grande-Terre, unaware that this busy West Indian trading center, recently seized by the British, had been even more recently recovered by the French. Arnold assumed the ships in its narrow harbor to be British. Discovering his mistake too late to turn back, he landed boldly and identified himself as an American merchant named John Anderson—an interesting touch since "John Anderson" was the fictional name Major André had used in the treason negotiations.

His masquerade was unsuccessful. Suspecting him of being English, the French hustled him aboard a prison ship in the harbor, thus setting in train the sequence of adventures that gives a last thrilling glimpse of the old Arnold, the daring, resourceful, and valiant Arnold of Quebec and Bemis Heights.

He had managed to hold on to his money—some £5,000 which he had brought for trading—and he soon put small amounts of it to good use as bribes. He learned that a British fleet was now blockading the harbor; he also heard that he was slated for the gallows. Further bribes to his guards put him in touch with the British flagship *Boyne* and procured the equipment he needed. On June 29, 1794, as the sultry, tropical evening became night and the tide turned, Arnold placed his money and other valuables in a cask and dropped it overboard—a gamble that worked,

Arnold, a merchant now, and Peggy knew little peace in this house in St. John, New Brunswick, where they lived from 1787 until a mob virtually ran them out of town in 1791.

for later the cask washed ashore below Pointe-à-Pitre, where a British landing force had encamped.

In the late dark hours, Arnold slid down a rope to a small raft that was waiting for him. On this he made his way to a rowboat that had been anchored in the harbor, and then pulled for the British fleet as fast—and as quietly—as he could. At one point he had to outrow a French cutter that hailed him: clever work with his own smaller, more maneuverable boat got him away in the darkness. At four o'clock in the morning the built-up shoe that Arnold wore on his shrunken wounded leg pounded the deck boards of the *Boyne*.

Off and on for the next two years he served as a volunteer officer under Sir Charles Grey, the general commanding the British land forces in the West Indies. He organized the supply service and acted as an agent for the British planters affected by the slow British retreat from Guadeloupe and other French West Indian possessions. Once more he tried to obtain a permanent and suitable post in the British Army. Once more his requests met with refusal; he told his wife that the British would not even let him seek a soldier's death.

Still, his last military efforts did not go unrewarded. A committee of West Indian planters and merchants drew up a resolution, thanking him for "beneficial" services. As a former Loyalist officer on half pay, he was granted 13,400 acres of Crown land in Quebec. This, however, did not provide him with immediate financial returns.

Dwindling finances were not the traitor's only problem. In 1795 Benedict, the eldest of his sons by his first

wife, died in Jamaica of gangrene, after being wounded while fighting with the British. In May of 1800, Sophia, his and Peggy's only daughter, had a paralytic stroke that left her a semi-invalid for life. A month later Edward, their favorite son, left for India as an officer in the British engineers. "His death," Peggy told sister Betsy, "could scarcely be a more severe stroke."

Even before Edward had completed the tedious five-months' voyage to his post at Cawnpore, Peggy was penning him a long letter, outlining the doleful state into which her husband's privateering ventures had fallen. Such "insignificant prizes" as Arnold's captains had taken, she complained, had caused her husband "more trouble than profit" because of the legal formalities involved in their condemnation. She added that the petty officers on her husband's ships were throwing out "some very broad hints that handsome fortunes have been made by ransoming Ships at sea, but as we have not proof we must sit down quietly with the loss. . . . [Arnold] is, at present, in the most harassed wretched state that I have ever seen him. Disappointed in his highly raised expectations, harassed by the Sailors who are loudly demanding their prize-money, when in fact their advances have greatly exceeded anything that is due to them, and wishing still to do something, without the health or power of acting, he knows not which way to turn himself." Peggy herself tended to much of her husband's business. Her own informed view was that Arnold's skippers had "done" him out of "about £50,000."

Most of this unhappy letter was written on January 14, 1801. A few weeks later Arnold's already broken health took a turn for the worse, following the renewal of a chronic cough contracted in the tropics. Gout attacked his unwounded leg; the other ached constantly, and he walked only with a cane. Overwhelmed by accumulated frustrations, he failed rapidly. His face became deeply wrinkled; only the blue eyes reminded his friends of the old Arnold.

In the early summer Peggy took him to Galleywood, near Chelmsford, to spend a week with her friends Ann and Sarah Fitch. The General seemed to improve in the country air, but following their return to London, he was much worse. His doctors' diagnosis was dropsy, and on June 10 he became delirious.

Legend has it that as death approached he called for his old American uniform and said he wished he had never removed it. Historians generally discredit this as inconsistent with his conviction that nothing he chose to do could be wrong. Quite possibly his only regrets were that he had failed to deliver West Point to the British, and that his lifelong struggle for fame and fortune had brought him only infamy and debts.

Arnold died at six thirty in the morning of Sunday,

June 14, 1801. With Napoleon scourging the continent, the London press had little space for the demise of an unpopular figure. The *Post*, violently at odds with the ministry headed by the younger Pitt, observed that "Poor General Arnold has departed this world without notice; a sorry reflection this for the Pitts and . . . other turncoats." *European Magazine* dismissed him as "a person much noticed during the American War." Although *Gentleman's Magazine* later ran a two-column obituary, its original account was brief. "Died," it read, "at his house in Gloucester-place, Brigadier-General Arnold. His remains were interred on the 21st at Brompton. Seven mourning-coaches and four state-carriages formed the cavalcade." Even this terse notice was in error. Arnold was not buried in Brompton. He rests today, as does Peggy, on the other side of the Thames in the crypt of the little copper-spired Church of St. Mary, Battersea.

Ann Fitch conveyed the details to Philadelphia. "My sister & myself were with Mrs. Arnold when her husband expired," she informed Judge Shippen, "she evinces upon this occasion—as you know she has done upon many trying ones before—that fortitude & resignation, which a superior & well regulated mind *only* is capable of exerting."

In truth Peggy's mind was just barely equal to the ordeal. That deep down she was a woman of extraordinary fortitude, all the known facts of her life attest. But her nerves lay close to the surface. The slightest jar set them to thrumming. When she was able to write her father, she confessed that the General's death had reduced her to a "despairing state." At one period, convinced that her wretchedness was embittering the lives of her children, she had considered suicide. To her brother-in-law, Edward Burd, she confided that "my sufferings are not of the present moment only,—Years of unhappiness have past, I had cast my lot, complaints were unavailing, and you and my other friends, are ignorant of the many causes of un-

Mr. Lomask is the author of Beauty and the Traitor: The Story of Mrs. Benedict Arnold, *published last spring by Macrae Smith.*

Principal source materials include the many letters of Peggy Shippen Arnold printed in The Pennsylvania Magazine of History and Biography, *1900–1902;* Letters and Papers Relating Chiefly to the Provincial History of Pennsylvania, *edited by Thomas Balch (Philadelphia, 1855); and* Some New Light on the Later Life and Last Resting Place of Benedict Arnold and of His Wife Margaret Shippen, *by George Taylor (George White, 1931). Of the many biographies of Arnold, Mr. Lomask found most useful* Traitorous Hero: The Life and Fortunes of Benedict Arnold, *by Willard M. Wallace (Harper and Brothers, 1954).*

easiness I have had." Yet a year after Arnold's death she was writing to her surviving stepsons in Canada, "Although I have suffered, in my choice of evils, almost beyond human endurance, I now repent not at having made it."

During the little stretch of life left to Peggy she managed to pay off every one of her husband's ascertainable debts. These, according to her own estimate, came to "upwards of £6,000." Her father helped her with occasional remittances, but she did most of it herself by stringent economies. She sold her furniture, moving from the handsome home on Gloucester Place to a cheaper one on nearby Bryanston Street. The furniture for this "small but very neat house" she purchased from a servant who, as she observed in one of her letters, "is now a more independent woman than her mistress."

Even as Peggy struggled with her late husband's obligations, she contrived to put her younger children in good schools and to help her older ones get a good start in life. Letter after letter bespeaks the intensity of her affection and concern for her "uncommonly excellent" sons and her "dear, handsome Sophia." In the dark months following Arnold's death she wrote her father that she was counting "my blessings"—four sons and a daughter who had never given her "a moment's uneasiness," whose goodness was "a never-failing source of delight."

All of them, as well as her stepsons in America, lived respectable and successful if not distinguished lives, unhindered by their father's reputation.

For years Peggy's health had been erratic. On July 3, 1803, she wrote her sister from Chambers Farm, Epping, a country home in Essex, that she had "been much of an invalid lately" and had "found it necessary to consult our two first medical men, in the female line, Doctors Denman & Clarke. They have ascertained it to be a complaint of the womb. . . . It is now several weeks since I have eaten animal food, or tasted wine, beer or any thing heating . . . and I am obliged to keep almost constantly in a recumbent posture." On November 2, 1803, she informed her father simply and forthrightly that the doctors had given a name to her "long-standing" illness. It was "a cancer," she told him in a short note written from London.

Suffering terribly, confined most of the time to a prone position, she continued to correspond with him. "I have been indeed very near death," she wrote on May 14, 1804; ". . . my complaints are such, as to give me little hope of long continuing an Inhabitant of this world. . . . I trust I bear this heavy affliction with great resignation; and I do not suffer my spirits to overcome me." On July 15 she wrote what appears to have been her last letter to her father:

...sincere thanks for your very acceptable present, which came most opportunely, having been obliged to incur a great many unavoidable expenses . . . [I am] constantly under the effects of opium, to relieve a pain which would otherwise be intolerable. . . . Mr. [Robert R.] Livingston, your Minister to Paris, called upon me several times during his stay in London, where he was not very well received. —He appears completely to have adopted French principles, and French ideas.—I have written this in great haste, and am always obliged to write while laying down, which is indeed almost wholly my position.—Pray remember me most tenderly to all the family, and believe me, my beloved Parent, most truly and affectionately

Yours
M. A.

Death came on August 24, 1804. She was only forty-four, but she had lived long enough to have been able to write her stepsons during the preceding summer, "To you I have rendered an essential service; I have rescued your Father's memory from disrespect, by paying all his just debts; and his Children will now never have the mortification of being reproached with his speculations having injured anybody beyond his own family. . . . I have not even a tea-spoon, a towel, or a bottle of wine that I have not paid for."

The note of quiet triumph was understandable. As a devoted wife and mother, faithful to her bargains and gallant under strain, the lovely Mrs. Benedict Arnold had made a good ending to an ill-starred life.

The Marianas Turkey Shoot CONTINUED FROM PAGE 29

down about twenty-four Zeros over the islands, destroying more on the fields at Iwo and Chichi. Off Chichi Jima my planes intercepted the 1,900-ton transport *Tatsutakawa Maru*. Over four hundred Japanese went over the side as the steamer burned. The destroyers *Boyd* and *Charrette* finally sank her, then proceeded to rescue all Japanese sailors who were willing to be picked up. The two ships rescued 118 people in all, but two of these changed their minds and jumped off the destroyers later. The 116 prisoners were delivered on board *Hornet*. Another sixteen picked up later made a total of 132 Japanese aboard my flagship, a record for the carriers.

While the Marines were landing on Saipan to the south, we attacked Chichi and Iwo. Our planes destroyed many of the choice targets—oil dumps, buildings, aircraft, and small vessels; we did not need Harrill, as it turned out, but he did assist by maintaining a combat air patrol. My planes also worked over the smaller island of Haha Jima.

Heavy weather developed by late afternoon, making recovery of our planes difficult. One crashed on the badly pitching *Belleau Wood*. It started a fire that looked serious, but Captain Jack Perry and his heroic crew put it out. The sea became so rough that I cancelled the remaining strikes, but I kept two night fighters over Chichi Jima during the night in order to heckle the Japanese and prevent their planes from taking off at dawn. Both task groups had retired to the south during the night, but we could not avoid the weather. The carriers were pitching too badly to launch any planes.

In the afternoon, as the wind abated somewhat, I launched a fighter sweep and two bombing strikes against Iwo Jima. They added to the destruction done

on the previous day. After the recovery of my planes, both task groups headed south. The mission had been a great success; we had destroyed for the time being the Japanese air threat from the north staged through the Bonin Islands, thereby protecting the invasion forces.

Meanwhile, bigger game was approaching the Marianas—the Japanese First Mobile Fleet, which according to our intelligence estimates included nine carriers with about 450 aircraft. During the next afternoon, June 17, Mitscher ordered us to send searches to the southwest. The position of the enemy fleet was known by our trailing submarines; possibly it could be hit later from two sides, if our planes spotted it. I sent twelve search planes 350 miles to the southwest, then steamed in that direction to recover them and be that much closer to the enemy. The result of the search was negative, because the Japanese fleet was still seven hundred miles away.

That night I faced an important decision; an opportunity was presented that seldom comes in the lifetime of a naval officer. Had I steamed to the southwestward all night, by the next morning I could place myself between the Japanese fleet and its homeland, thereby blocking off its retreat and boxing in the enemy between our four task groups. I called Harrill on the TBS [special inter-ship] voice radio and explained the situation to him. I also called Rear Admiral Ralph Davison, who was riding in "makee learn," or training, status on board *Yorktown*. Davison strongly endorsed my idea, but Harrill would have nothing to do with it, maintaining that his orders were to rendezvous with Mitscher the next morning west of Saipan. He told me he had had enough of independent operations and was now going to make his rendezvous. Without further ado, he changed course and headed off to the south, leaving me all alone. I dared not break radio silence to consult Mitscher, for this would have disclosed my position to the Japanese fleet.

My staff and I discussed the alternatives. Conceivably, the Japanese might have concentrated on me before the trap was set and possibly sunk some of my ships. With Harrill, our two task groups had three hundred fighters and two hundred attack planes, which I considered more than a match for the entire enemy carrier force. But when Harrill sailed away, he took some ninety fighters and seventy bombers with him. I did not wish to find myself on a windy corner with so many Japanese airplanes that I could not shoot them all down. In addition, embarking on my own course might have embarrassed Mitscher in front of Spruance; I admired both men, but it was obvious to me that Spruance did not understand the full capabilities of the fast carriers. Together, Mitscher's fifteen carriers made a virtually invincible force. If Mitscher had been in command of the Fifth Fleet, I would have continued to the southwest. But Mitscher was subordinate to Spruance, and I did not want to disturb their good working relationship. Finally, I asked myself if I were not about to take the whole world on my shoulders.

In many ways, my situation recalled the Battle of Jutland in 1916. Vice Admiral David Beatty made a similar decision in the opening stages of that celebrated fleet action of World War I. Beatty had been racing toward the enemy fleet with his fast battle cruisers, trying to get behind the German battle force to prohibit its retreat and box it in between his force and the British Grand Fleet under Admiral John R. Jellicoe. Beatty was out of touch with Jellicoe and made his dash without keeping Jellicoe adequately informed. His boldness made him the hero of that war, but he lost two of his ships and was almost caught by the German High Seas Fleet. He could have lost the battle. In 1925, Admiral J. M. "Billy Goat" Reeves, who was a great student of Jutland, gave a four-hour lecture on the battle at his headquarters in San Diego.

Cover for the enemy fleet was provided by the Zero.

Aireview, TOKYO

Reeves's conclusion was that Beatty made a mistake in trying to trap the Germans without keeping Jellicoe informed. My friend Lieutenant Al Buehler, who had listened with me, summarized Reeves's lecture in three words, "Beatty bitches battle!" Now I applied Buehler's remark to my own situation.

After debating the pros and cons, my staff and I decided against striking off on our own, so I turned, following Harrill, to carry out my orders. Later, after the Marianas were captured, Mitscher told me he thought I should have continued to the southwest to get behind the Japanese fleet. He uttered practically the same words Admiral Ernest J. King had said to me when I had wanted to attack Rabaul very early in the war, "I almost ordered you to do it." So I missed the chance of becoming the Beatty of World War II. But the enemy had not yet closed, and there was still an opportunity to deal a crushing blow to the Japanese fleet. I rejoined the other three task groups off Guam on the morning of June 18, fully expecting Admiral Spruance to assume tactical command and head west to attack the Japanese fleet. But he did not. Conflicting or vague submarine reports suggested that two Japanese forces were approaching, as had been the case during the Midway campaign. One force was known to be due west of Guam, the other possibly southwest; consequently, Spruance kept the carriers off Guam as a shield for the exposed southern flank of our landing forces at Saipan, awaiting better reports of enemy movements. The Japanese fleet was still about seven hundred miles away from the Fifth Fleet, which meant no battle could be joined that day.

In the morning, the destroyer *Cowell* picked up sixteen survivors from the Japanese transport *Shinjiki Maru*, which had been sunk six days before by Harrill's planes. Later, my combat air patrol shot down a snooper 250 miles northwest of the formation, probably from the Jimas. We spent the day cruising back and forth near Guam, sending aircraft searches to the southwest.

During the night, Spruance was faced with the decision of whether or not to go west. It became evident that the Japanese held a theoretical advantage. They could launch their carrier planes from six hundred miles out, attack the Fifth Fleet, land and refuel on Guam, attack us again, and fly back to their carriers. We could not reach their carriers if we remained near the Marianas. The maximum operating radius of our planes was 350 miles, which meant we had to continue westward during the night to get within combat range of the Japanese for strikes the next morning. Spruance's great concern was the protection of the invasion forces. He was afraid of an "end run." The transports could have been protected just as well from 250 miles farther west, with our radar, our search planes, and our submarines keeping us informed of the movements of the enemy fleet.

At 8 P.M. Spruance ordered the fleet to head eastward, which we had to do anyway in order to operate aircraft, since the wind was from the east. This was definitely not closing the Japanese fleet. In my judgment, we should have steamed west at every opportunity. At midnight, Admiral Mitscher recommended that the fleet turn west to meet the enemy because at 10 P.M. a radio-direction-finder report had placed the Japanese fleet 355 miles to the west. Spruance, however, persisted in remaining near the invasion forces and sent a message at 12:38 A.M., June 19, to Mitscher: "End run by other fast ones remains a possibility and must not be overlooked."

At first light, Mitscher ordered me to launch a special 325-mile search to the southwest, which I did, with negative results. *Hornet* was on the eastern end of Task Force 58, and at daylight I could actually see Guam on the horizon. At 6:19 Spruance ordered all carrier task groups to change course westward in the general direction of the Japanese fleet.

U.S. carrier, Essex class

A few snoopers had been splashed by the other groups, but not until 7:05 did my group get into the act. Lieutenant Charlie Ridgway detected many airplanes over Guam on his radar screen and dispatched four night fighters to investigate. Finding a number of Japanese planes in a landing circle over Guam, these Hellcats immediately went to work. I ordered twenty-four more fighters sent to Guam, then reported to Mitscher. Mitscher radioed all task groups: "Send fighter assistance to Guam immediately." My acknowledgement was: "Help is on the way." These Japanese planes were unquestionably from the approaching fleet. Lieutenant Russell Reiserer, leading the night fighters, tore into the Japanese planes at Guam. Other Hellcats, mostly from my task group, assisted. Enemy planes that were not destroyed in the air were shot up on the ground after landing. Reiserer himself scored five kills, which he modestly reported to me on the flag bridge upon his return. On my recommendation, Mitscher gave him the Navy Cross for becoming an ace.

At 9 A.M. Owen Sowerwine, my communications officer, intercepted a corrected contact report from a PBM Mariner search plane whose previous message, several hours earlier, had been garbled. The report pinpointed the Japanese fleet over 360 miles away, still beyond the range of our aircraft. We relayed the message to Mitscher, who sent it on to Spruance.

Task Force 58 was steaming west but getting nowhere, since the carriers had to swing around to the east to launch planes. At 9:37 Ridgway and the other

task group combat intelligence officers began to pick up aircraft on their radars 130 miles to the westward. Mitscher recalled all his fighters from Guam to defend the carriers, ordering all dive bombers and torpedo planes to take off and orbit east of Guam. This expedient kept the carrier decks free to land, service, and launch fighters. At 10:04 general quarters was sounded, and all hands in the force went to their battle stations. Meanwhile, 450 Hellcats and a few night F4U Corsairs took off to intercept the attacking Japanese.

The melee that followed was aptly described by one pilot as "the Marianas Turkey Shoot." Our pilots and planes were so superior to those of Japan that only a handful of enemy planes reached our ships, and these were promptly shot down by antiaircraft fire. Throughout the day, the Japanese repeatedly tried to launch air strikes against our ships, but each time our pilots shot the enemy out of the sky.

Our operations took Task Force 58 even closer to Guam. Mitscher knew the Japanese were trying to land there, so he ordered the bombers that were orbiting east of Guam to drop their charges on the airfield, and the bomb craters they produced caused a number of Japanese planes to crash. The desperate enemy pilots fought savagely to defend the integrity of Guam as their one refuge. We lost several pilots there toward evening, but by nightfall Guam was quiet; the last snoopers had turned away before eight o'clock.

Reports of the battle were impressive. My pilots claimed 109 enemy planes shot down, while the total for Task Force 58 turned out to be 385. It was the greatest aerial victory in the Pacific war. Forty Hellcats were lost, but many of the pilots were rescued. The Japanese lost about eleven aviators to every one of ours, a ratio that continued throughout the war. Admiral Mitscher sent a message to all hands: "The aviators and gun ships of this task force have done a job today which will make their country proud of them. Their skillful defense of this task force enabled the force to escape a vicious, well-coordinated aircraft attack carried out with determination."

Admiral Spruance was not convinced that the Japanese air attack was spent until 10 P.M., when Task Force 58 took its last plane aboard. Then, at last, he headed toward the enemy fleet. At that stage we were forty miles from Guam, so closing the enemy became a long stern chase, but since the backbone of enemy air strength was expended, we possessed an overwhelming advantage once we got within aircraft range. As a precaution, I topped off [refueled] my destroyers. Just then I heard Admiral Harrill ask Mitscher if his task group could stay behind, because it was low on fuel. My big ships had the same amount of fuel as Harrill's, but he had not topped off his destroyers, so Mitscher left him behind. I immediately signalled Mitscher: "Would greatly appreciate remaining with you. We have plenty of fuel." He replied that my task group would remain with him until the battle ended. To me this was a compliment, but it also indicated Mitscher's growing impatience with Harrill. Task Group 58.4 had broken away at 1 P.M. and continued to hit Guam, and then refueled the next day. "Harrill fought this group well through the Marianas 'Turkey Shoot,'" historian Samuel Eliot Morison later wrote, "but came down with appendicitis 28 June and was then relieved...."

Task Force 58 steamed west at twenty-three knots during the night. While the pilots of Task Force 58 slept, the plane mechanics prepared the aircraft for the battle expected the next day. As we passed over the waters of the afternoon air battles, one of my destroyers picked up three of our airmen floating in a life raft. At first light we launched a long-range search flight 325 miles to the west, but these planes found nothing to report. Around 9 A.M. our combat air patrol shot down three snoopers. We pressed on, but sighted no enemy ships.

The quiet of this Sunday afternoon at sea was suddenly broken at 3:40 by excited chatter over the radio. The Japanese fleet had been sighted 275 miles due west of Saipan, steaming northwest at twenty knots. Eight minutes later Mitscher told all task groups to report to him any other radio messages they heard. At 3:53 he gave us the word: "Expect to launch everything we have, probably have to recover at night." The pilots, who had been in their ready rooms since dawn, now copied down the latest target information from the ticker-tape screens onto their navigation charts. Mitscher gave them a parting thought: "The primary mission is to get the carriers." At 4:10 the pilots manned their planes, and at 4:21 we turned into the wind to execute a record ten-minute launch.

The flight consisted of 216 planes—eighty-five Hellcats, fifty-four Avengers, fifty-one SB2C Helldivers, and twenty-six SBD Dauntlesses. But no sooner was the strike on its way than the search planes sent in a corrected position report placing the Japanese fleet sixty miles farther west. This meant that our planes had to fly 335 miles to the target, attack the enemy fleet before darkness, and fly back to the carriers in the dark. The trip and attack would amount to over seven hundred miles of flying, which was about the limit of fuel. Some planes would surely have to land in the water at night. Those pilots whose fuel lasted could land aboard, but unfortunately none of them

had qualified for night carrier landings. This was a sample of Mitscher's indomitable leadership. He gambled despite the expected losses, knowing full well that this was our one and only chance to hit the Japanese fleet.

At this point in the battle I realized bitterly what a great opportunity I had missed on June 18 by not getting behind the Japanese fleet. Retreat would have been impossible, for my carriers would have stood between it and the homeland, making this precarious flight unnecessary. In the game of war an advantage unpressed may have tragic consequences. To me this seemed to be a case in point.

Around 7 P.M., as a half-hour air attack on the Japanese warships was ending in approaching darkness, we began to get reports from our planes. Antiaircraft fire was thick; the battleships and cruisers in desperation fired their heavy guns at our planes. About seventy-

U.S. carrier, Independence *class*

five Japanese fighters took off from the carriers, and our Hellcats attacked them immediately. By Japanese records, only ten of their planes survived. Racing against the sudden tropical darkness, our pilots executed hastily co-ordinated attacks on the flaming ships. Planes from *Belleau Wood* in my task group succeeded in sinking one carrier, *Hiyo*. Lieutenant (j.g.) George P. Brown flew down along the flight deck to draw away antiaircraft fire, thus allowing Lieutenant (j.g.) Warren R. Omark to drop his torpedo into the ship's side. Unfortunately, the courageous Brown went into the sea on the return flight and was never found. Some bombs hit and damaged the carriers *Zuikaku* and *Junyo*, but they managed to limp back to the homeland.

Pitch-black darkness had already descended as the running lights of the first of our returning planes appeared over the horizon. With understandable anxiety, for I had flown at night from carriers myself, I made a drastic decision. I ordered all my ships to turn on all their lights. Of course, this was taking a chance that no enemy submarines were lurking nearby. To identify my task group I ordered *Hornet* to display in addition a vertical searchlight beam. I notified Admiral Mitscher of my action at once, and he promptly signified his approval by ordering all the ships of the entire task force to turn on their lights. This was indeed one of the war's supreme moments— a multitude of ships emblazed the skies for many miles in a calculated risk to provide greater safety for the return of battle-worn airmen.

The assistant air officer of *Yorktown*, Lieutenant Commander Verne W. Harshman, rigged a cargo light to shine down on the flight deck to facilitate landings. Other ships then used this innovation to advantage.

Flown by Commander Bill Dean, skipper of Fighting 2, the first Hellcat landed aboard *Hornet*. Dean rushed up to the bridge to report the results of the attack and expressed great fear that he was going to lose many of his fine pilots in the recovery operation. I tried to allay his apprehension, and, as it turned out, he did not lose a single man.

Recovery of the returning planes, however, was a wild scramble, as the exhausted pilots rushed to get on board before their fuel gave out. We ordered them to land on any carrier they could find. Some deck crashes fouled flight decks for a few minutes, but very few flight personnel were injured. Many planes landed in the water, but destroyers picked up the pilots and crews. Everyone concentrated on rescue operations. During all this activity, Sol Phillips radioed that a Japanese Zero was circling *Oakland*. Thinking it was one of our carrier planes trying to land, I asked him: "How do you know it's Japanese?"

He signalled back: "I can tell by the red balls on its wings!"

Lieutenant Michael S. Alexatos, returning in a Hellcat, heard over the plane's radio circuit: "Hey, that was a Jap Zero!" Since it was not seen again, it must have ditched in the sea.

Knowing he was low on fuel, Alexatos asked for the location of his ship, *Yorktown*. The reply was: "We are the one with the searchlight turned straight up."

He headed for the first searchlight he saw, because his gasoline gauge read zero. He made a perfect landing, taxiing clear of the barrier. The engine of his plane sputtered and stopped. As he was climbing out of his cockpit, someone said, "Welcome aboard *Hornet*."

The mistake was understandable, since *Hornet* and *Yorktown* each had a searchlight turned straight up.

Task Force 58 steamed over the path of the returning flight during the night picking up more downed pilots. The final count of our task force losses on June 19 and 20 was one hundred airplanes, sixteen pilots, thirty-three aircrewmen, and, due to deck crashes, two ship's officers and four enlisted men. Postwar investigation revealed that Japan, in contrast, lost three carriers, including two sunk by submarines before June 19, and 445 aircraft, including twelve catapult planes from battleships and cruisers, along with about fifty land-based planes destroyed at Guam. The Japanese fleet still had aircraft carriers left, but only about ten planes aboard them, so if we had come within striking distance we would have encountered negligible air opposition. As we tried to chase the fleet through the next night and throughout the following day, June 21, our extreme-range scouting planes sighted the fleeing ships intermittently, but they were always beyond our combat radius. We did not have fuel in our ships to pursue the enemy farther west.

The two-day engagement that was fought west of Guam, in the direction of the Philippine Islands, became known as the Battle of the Philippine Sea and thus gave a name to the area. The first day, in the Marianas Turkey Shoot, we broke the backbone of the Japanese carrier air strength. The second day we inflicted damage on seventeen of their ships, including the sinking of *Hiyo*. Because it was Mitscher's one and only opportunity to strike the Japanese, it was called "Mitscher's Sunday Punch."

On my track charts I wrote the words made famous by Horace Greeley: "Go West, young man, go West," which in my opinion is what Admiral Spruance should have done on the night of June 18.

The naval analyst must examine dispassionately all aspects of a naval engagement. Through the pages of history, major wars have often been decided by the outcome of a single battle, as in the case of Salamis or Actium. The naval commander is at his best when he takes full advantage of every chance to destroy his enemy. The bigger the battle, the better the naval officer. It is a fair statement to say that had we sunk every Japanese ship the war might have ended in days instead of in fifteen months. Spruance could still have provided maximum protection for the invasion forces even if his carriers had been farther west on the morning of June 19, and the airfields at Guam and Rota could have been kept inoperative just as well from that position. It was not possible for the approaching Japanese fleet to make "end runs" around our aircraft carriers. Had we been two hundred miles farther west that morning, we could have scored a decisive naval victory.

My high admiration for Spruance has been maintained ever since he was my first destroyer skipper aboard the *Aaron Ward* in 1919. He won the crucial Battle of Midway, he blazed a trail across the Pacific from Tarawa to Saipan, and now in the Battle of the Philippine Sea he had turned back the Japanese fleet with staggering losses, without losing a single ship of his own. The tactical decisions he made as commander of the Fifth Fleet during this battle have been supported by historian Morison and by Admiral King, and I hesitate to align myself against such stalwarts. Yet the inescapable fact remains that our lost opportunity allowed the Japanese fleet to sail away, to fight again at the Battle for Leyte Gulf.

The Life and Death of a Great Newspaper

Horace Greeley founded the "Trib"—and the union that eventually helped kill it. But in 125 years it knew many a shining hour

By FRED C. SHAPIRO

NATIONAL PORTRAIT GALLERY

It was ten on Saturday evening, April 23, 1966, when M. C. (Inky) Blackman, a short, gray-haired rewrite man, put a ticktacktoe mark at the bottom of a news story, stood up, grunted good night, and without further ceremony left the fifth floor of the building at 230 West Forty-first Street, New York City. Although he didn't know it at the time, the endmark on Blackman's piece also wrote finis to a great newspaper that had once been America's greatest newspaper. After 125 years and 43,483 daily issues, the New York *Tribune*—since 1924 the New York *Herald Tribune*—was lapsing into a labor paralysis from which it would never recover. The paper's final publisher, John Hay Whitney, whose golden touch had awed the oil and chemical industries, had struggled vainly for eight years with the *Herald Tribune*—and had lost an estimated twenty million dollars. The *Herald Tribune* never resumed publication. On August 15, 114 days after its last edition, it was pronounced dead. Its Sunday paper and certain elements of its format were merged into the ill-omened *World Journal Tribune*, which itself lingered for less than eight months before following its three parent papers into oblivion. But of all the thirteen pa-

Thomas Nast made this caricature of Horace Greeley in 1872; here it is superimposed on a facsimile of the Tribune's first edition.

pers, morning and afternoon, liberal and conservative, whose legacies were merged in that unfortunate salvage attempt, there was none whose accomplishments or influence could rival Horace Greeley's "Try-bune," once known in a simpler time as "the bible of the West."

The New York *Tribune* sprang into existence on April 10, 1841, on $2,000 capital—$1,000 of it borrowed. Its editor was an inconsistent and volatile New England printer, already growing bald at thirty, who had graduated to the publication of what were primarily Whig political papers and pamphlets, as well as a magazine with literary pretensions, the *New Yorker* (no relation, of course, to the urbane magazine of today).

The paper he founded at 30 Ann Street, a ramshackle two-story building near the base of Manhattan, was in competition politically with four Whig papers already in existence, the *Courier and Enquirer*, the *American*, the *Express*, and the *Commercial Advertiser*—but there would be a difference. The established Whig papers sold at six cents per day, or ten dollars to yearly subscribers; Greeley would peg the *Tribune*'s price to compete with the two brawling brothers of the "penny press," the *Sun*, established by Benjamin Day in 1833, and the *Herald*, first published by James Gordon Bennett in 1835. In the *Tribune*, however, Greeley promised in a prepublication prospectus:

"The immoral and degrading police reports, advertisements and other matter which have been allowed to disgrace the columns of our leading penny papers will be carefully excluded from this, and no exertion will be spared to render it worthy of the hearty approval of the virtuous and refined, and a welcome visitant at the family fireside."

A paper for the "virtuous and refined" at a price that appealed to the American laborer was a contradictory undertaking, but then Horace Greeley is undoubtedly the most contradictory figure to spring—in two directions at once—into American journalism and American history. He supported, and then denounced—and on occasion, supported and denounced again—propositions and personages from aldermen to Presidents. The first *Tribune* editorial Greeley wrote was in praise of John Tyler; yet seven months later the editor announced two presidential post-office nominations by

listing them under the heading "Appointments by Judas Iscariot." Equally contradictory, perhaps, was Greeley's attitude toward the hard-working American workingman he claimed to represent. A founder and the first president of the New York Printers' Union (later Typographical Union Number Six), he paid *Tribune* printers thirty-two cents for each 1,000 ems set in type when other papers were paying twenty-three; in 1844, the editor led the battle for a higher city-wide scale for printers, and won. The victory was celebrated by the firing of a cannon in front of the *Tribune* office. On the other hand, Greeley thundered his denunciation of the other side of the unionization coin, the right to strike. In its earlier days particularly, the *Tribune* generally ignored the existence of strikes —and even distorted what little news its editor allowed to be printed about them. "I don't want to encourage these lawless proceedings," Greeley explained. Yet, although he frequently quarrelled with his printers—once even hiring strikebreakers—Greeley remained, generally, on good terms with them. In 1862, just a year after they had refused to accept a ten per cent pay cut announced by the editor, *Tribune* printers chipped in to purchase Greeley a $400 gold watch.

Squabbles with his printers, and $400 gold watches for that matter, were a long time away, however, on what the editor later described as the "cold, clammy morning" when he first published his "new Morning Journal of Politics, Literature and General Intelligence." On the back page of this hopeful first issue, the printers were directed to turn the rules to effect a black-bordered sign of mourning where Greeley described the city's funeral honors for President Harrison, whose term of office had been cut short at one month by the pneumonia he contracted at his inauguration. For the first of his four pages, though,

Greeley offered a powerful attraction: the text, in full, of a decision by the attorney general of New York declaring New York City Recorder Robert H. Morris guilty of "manifest usurpation of power." On the two inside pages Greeley and his editorial staff of two, Henry J. Raymond and George M. Snow, denounced Recorder Morris at length, and railed at the sharp two-year increase of $67,000 in almshouse expenditures. There were also a few financial items, as well as a table of quotations on the money market and a stock table that listed all eighteen issues on the New York Stock Exchange. That first edition, printed on two flat-bed presses, comprised 5,000 papers, and Greeley, who had managed to enlist only 500 advance subscribers, considered himself fortunate to be able to give away the unsold copies.

A typical day's coverage in the first year included articles dealing with a demonstration at Tammany Hall; a meeting of the Bible Society; a session of the committee investigating the affairs of Columbia College; a meeting to devise measures for improvement of the lot of the Negro population; a temperance parade; sessions of the board of aldermen, the commissioners of emigration, and the commissioners of taxes, as well as the proceedings of a trial for murder; the particulars of seven fires; a review of the opera; and thirteen other items, chiefly of marine and financial interest. There were no sports items, per se, in those first issues; it was not until the twenty-fourth issue that Greeley grudgingly gave space to the proceedings of a ball game. The result must have been gratifying, for a few weeks later sports invaded page one with a story about a "ball play game between Bulexe and the Choktaw Indians." For the record, the Choktaws won and collected, in wagers, the possessions—including the clothing—of the defeated team.

Early days, noted writers: Assistant Henry Raymond and Managing Editor Charles A. Dana (in profile, right) helped Greeley's paper survive its infancy. Literary pieces had wide appeal, as did Taylor's foreign reporting, Marx's letters from Europe, and Margaret Fuller's lively reviews. "California News— Reading the Tribune*" (far right) was a plug for the sheet's coast-to-coast news coverage.*

CULVER

Henry J. Raymond

Excepting possibly the scanty sports accounts, however, there seemed no item small or insignificant enough to escape the moralizing of the editor, including the reports of the frequent temperance meetings. "We trust that the convincing arguments for total abstinence will have a good effect," Greeley would close such an account. "They ought to at least." Not all of his comments made dull reading. Witness the full text of the column of Washington news printed in the *Tribune* on Christmas Day 1852: "Congress did nothing yesterday—to speak of."

Whatever the reason—the politics, the coverage, or the writing—circulation did pick up, and this despite the nation's first recorded circulation war. Owners of the *Sun* had instructed their newsboys to thrash any boys found selling the *Tribune*, but after six weeks Greeley nonetheless found himself able to sell 11,000 *Tribunes* on each of the six publishing days of the week. Advertising also increased, but at first profits failed to keep pace. In its initial week, the *Tribune* took in $92 but paid out $525. It continued to lose money at the rate of between $200 and $300 a week until, three months after the paper first came out, Greeley was able to persuade Thomas McElrath, an attorney with publishing experience, to invest $2,000 for a partnership.

The *Tribune*, Greeley had promised, would be dedicated among other things to furthering total abstinence from liquor ("Anti-Slavery, Anti-War, Anti-Rum, Anti-Tobacco, Anti-Seduction, Anti-Grogshops, Brothels, Gambling Houses"), but McElrath, and the hard facts of publishing life, soon managed to persuade Greeley to turn away from his noble intentions. Even more numerous than the liquor advertisements that romped through the columns of the paper were the advertisements for what appeared to be a myriad assortment of patent medicines. Worse, all the advertisements were

not necessarily contained in the advertising columns. By the sixth month of its existence the *Tribune*'s news columns were marred by paid items, or obvious commercial plugs for advertisers. There was, for instance, the "news item" announcing: "L. N. Fowler, our Practical Phrenologist, delivers tonight the finishing lecture of his present courses, and from the subject we venture to say that it will be as interesting and useful as any of the preceding discourses. See advertisement."

The money was beginning to come in, however—enough to allow the *Tribune* editor to invest some of his unaccustomed profits in the gathering of news; reporters and departments were added. The *Tribune* began paying more attention to finance, particularly real-estate transactions, which Greeley watched with a speculative eye, and to ship news. More important to the working-class readers he was seeking to attract, however, was the appearance of fiction—and poetry; the name of H. W. Longfellow was signed to a number of the early submissions. Greeley's taste in fiction ran, at first, to serialized stories from *Godey's Lady's Book*, but later he published chapters from Charles Dickens' *Barnaby Rudge* as they arrived from England. And despite Greeley's promised ban, a column of "City Intelligence" was installed in the paper.

If the *Tribune* had, by the simple pressure of economic survival, been forced to catch up with the rest of the town on the routine facets of journalism, it did, on Greeley's own initiative, spring ahead of them on the subject closest to his heart: politics. The paper astounded the pre-telegraphic city one morning by printing the summary of a speech that Daniel Webster had made only the day before in Boston. To accomplish this unprecedented feat, Greeley had dispatched his chief assistant, Raymond, and a crew of *Tribune* compositors to establish what

was, in essence, a water-borne composing room aboard the night boat to Boston. Raymond covered the speech and dashed back in time to catch the boat; during the night the printers hand-set the type as the reporter wrote the copy. The boat docked at 5 A.M., and the *Tribune* was on the street an hour later with the speech.

The principal method of obtaining news from other cities, before the formation of the Associated Press in 1848, was to lift it from papers that were mailed to New York in exchange for the local papers, and the pages of the early *Tribune* were sprinkled with such gleanings. Exchanges, however, were not sufficient for Greeley. Whenever possible, he wanted the *Tribune* to have its own men on the scene. This proved to be an expensive proposition, but correspondents were recruited in large cities here and abroad, including a Washington reporter whose identity is still screened by his pen name, Argus. At the same time, Greeley found a way to spread his expenses. Two of his previous publications, the *Log Cabin* (a relic of Harrison's "log cabin and hard cider" campaign of 1840) and the *New Yorker*, were merged to form a weekly edition of the *Tribune* that would contain a collection of Greeley's choicest daily fulminations, emphasizing particularly those with interest outside of New York. The *Weekly Tribune* would be mailed upstate and to Pennsylvania, Ohio, and the West, where newspapers were thus far unable to fill the demands of readers for national or foreign news.

The first *Weekly Tribune*, published five months after the birth of its parent paper, was a mixed bag. President Tyler's second veto message rubbed shoulders with "Eleanora," a short story by Edgar Allen Poe; "the address of the Whig membership of the Congress of the United States"; an article on "the New Revenue Law"; a column of "Doings in Washington";

Bayard Taylor

H. W. Longfellow

Edgar Allan Poe

Karl Marx

Margaret Fuller

and editorials on "Cabinet Changes" and the "Law of River Navigation." The success of the *Weekly Tribune* surprised even its ebullient editor. In twenty years' time, it was to build to a circulation of 200,000, the highest in the United States.

In the meantime, the daily *Tribune* had its successes. Four months after its first issue Greeley was complaining that twelve of his twenty daily columns were being pre-empted by advertising, and, after six months, he responded by expanding the paper from five to six columns per page. At the end of the first year, with circulation standing at 10,000, he expressed his satisfaction in glowing terms:

"Through one year, we have labored with whatever capacity we possess and with untiring assiduity to issue and establish a paper which should recommend itself to the approval of the virtuous, the enlightened, the enquiring, and the patriotic. Whatever errors we have committed have not been those of indolence or indifference.

"We have labored with whatever success to inculcate and advocate truth in each department of Political and Moral obligation and to publish a cheap paper which should furnish early and lucidly the NEWS of the day, and be at once an aid to the man of business and a welcome visitor to the fireside of every virtuous family. The extent to which our paper has commended itself to the favor and support of the public has fully equalled our most sanguine expectations."

And, apparently, it had. Thumbing his nose at the *Herald* and the *Sun*, Greeley raised the daily *Tribune*'s price to two cents and, reassured of its success, proceeded with plans to move it from the small Ann Street building to a new location at the junction of Nassau and Spruce streets and Park Row, across from City Hall, a site and structure owned by Mc-Elrath's father-in-law, Thompson Price.

The *Tribune* remained at this location—although not in that particular building —for nearly seventy-nine years. A fire in 1845 forced Greeley to return the *Tribune* to Ann Street to share the plant facilities of the *World* (it is one of the wonders of nineteenth-century journalism that papers brawling and feuding in their columns would, in emergencies, make every effort to assist each other), but the *Tribune* soon returned to its new site in a squat, five-story building that was purchased from Price in 1858 for $163,000. This building, as a *Tribune* brochure later boasted, possessed stairs "worn with the feet of men whom the future historian of this country will place among the most venerable figures in the most critical period of the American Republic."

The brochure (printed expressly for the centennial celebration of the nation's independence, held in Philadelphia) was not far wrong. From the new building Greeley waged his incessant campaigns: for reform and retrenchment in government; against alcohol, tobacco, and slaveholding; in favor of Associationism, (a modified form of Socialism propounded by the Frenchman Charles Fourier and his American disciple, Albert Brisbane, who proposed dividing society into "phalanxes" or joint stock companies); in favor of Transcendentalism (with exceptions); and in favor of high tariff protection (without exceptions).

To aid him in these campaigns, Greeley set out to build a staff that he could trust the paper to during what would prove to be frequent absences. Raymond, who was making $1,000 a year as assistant in the departments of literary criticism, fine arts, and general intelligence, soon defected and went over to feud with Greeley as managing editor of the *Courier and Enquirer*. (A few years later, in 1851, he started a paper of his own and called it the *New York Times*.) At the *Tribune* he was eventually suc-

ceeded by Charles A. Dana, who was to make something of a name for himself in journalism, too. It was Dana who took the initiative in building up the *Tribune* staff, hiring and assigning correspondents, including a man in London named Karl Marx, who wrote dispatches to the *Tribune* at one pound apiece for more than ten years. The author of the *Communist Manifesto*, the *Tribune* noted editorially, "has indeed opinions of his own, with some of which we are far from agreeing, but those who do not read his letters neglect one of the most instructive sources of information on the great questions of European politics." (See "When Karl Marx Worked for Horace Greeley" in the April, 1957, AMERICAN HERITAGE.)

During the *Tribune*'s early years, Greeley was not the easiest man to work for, but Dana, who put in fifteen years— as city editor, foreign correspondent, and finally as managing editor—made a fine complement for his querulous employer. He also showed a remarkable capacity to take direction from the Senior Editor, who was anything but tolerant of the weaknesses of subordinates. (On one occasion, angered by an error in proofreading, Greeley directed a subordinate editor to "oblige me and go upstairs and choke that infernal fool for nine minutes.") In addition to keeping a watchful eye on what appeared in the paper, Greeley insisted on having the final say on who worked for it—and on the salaries they were paid. Still, Greeley and Dana worked well together. As the latter's biographer, James H. Wilson, noted:

"Nothing seems to have been too trivial, or too great, for that matter, for their consideration. Standing, as it were, like sentinels on a watch tower, they caught the first signs of every social or political disturbance, and took cognizance of every event which promised to affect the public

George W. Smalley

interest. They were leaders, not followers, of public opinion . . ."

His mind eased, to some extent, over the editing of the *Tribune*, Greeley could now turn his attention to ridding himself of some of the more onerous tasks of publishing it, and, in 1849, he found his solution. Influenced somewhat by his Associationist leanings, he turned the paper into a joint-stock venture, issuing 100 shares of stock, each valued at $1,000. But apparently the teachings of Associationism had not found favor among the members of the *Tribune* staff, for only six employees came forward at the first offering with the courage—and the $1,000 —to invest in the *Tribune*. Of the other 94 shares, 10 were reserved for Dana, 31½ for Greeley, and 52½ for McElrath. Greeley, who was assured by the Tribune Association bylaws of an annual salary of $2,500, had thus surrendered nominal control of the paper, but until the last days of his life, even at times when he himself possessed only six shares, he never lost the decisive voice.

The formation of the association gave Greeley some of the freedom he was straining for, and so, he soon found, did the invention of the magnetic telegraph in 1845. With the subsequent linking of cables between the major cities, the pace of news in the papers picked up. The *Herald* was the first paper to capitalize on the telegraph in New York, but the *Tribune* quickly followed—not, however, without some misgivings on the part of its editor, who wrote in 1851: "In old days when there was no Telegraph and no Railroad between this city and New Haven, we used to arrange our expresses from that state so as to have the returns from two thirds of the towns in our office within ten hours from the close of the polls, and so tell how the state had gone in our next morning paper, but never since we have had two or three tele-graphic lines through that state have we been able to give a clear account of any election on the morning after its occurrence. . . ."

Though he grumbled about the new-fangled device, it enabled Greeley to exercise a kind of remote control over the *Tribune*, and, at the same time, to embark on his life's true work—lecturing, in and out of the paper, the American people. Now he could make long speaking tours and serve in the House of Representatives (where he was something less than a success, trying fruitlessly, as New York's Senator William H. Seward observed, "to reform Congress all at once"). He was also free to play a leading role in the formation of the Republican Party and, eventually, to prepare the free states for the break that would widen into civil war.

During the intervals when he did find himself at Park Row, however, Greeley enjoyed nothing more than the professional brawls that enlivened the journalism of his day. Not immune himself to libel problems (James Fenimore Cooper had won a $200 verdict against the *Tribune* in its first year), he took a particular delight in publicizing the libel difficulties of his rival, Bennett, whom he termed in print "the low-mouthed, blatant, witless, brutal proprietor of that sewer sheet." And even the gentlest of questions directed toward the Greeley theories was enough to bring down the wrath of the *Tribune*'s editor. Nettled when William Cullen Bryant, the poet-editor of the *Evening Post*, intimated that he had once been mild in his opposition to slavery, Greeley replied in the *Tribune*: "You lie, villain! Willfully, wickedly, basely lie!" And if he couldn't find a pretext for a quarrel, Greeley invented one. His way of celebrating the installation of a new font of type at the *Tribune* in 1846 was to editorialize, "If there be one thing that we dislike above all others, it is a flimsy, chocolate colored, half illegible, pitch-forked-together apology for a newspaper —like the *Express*, for example."

In this climate the *Tribune* flourished or declined—primarily the former—in relation to the popular reception of its editor. When Greeley backed prohibition and tax-supported public schools, the paper's circulation in liberal and Roman Catholic homes fell off markedly. As friction over the slavery question increased, however, circulation began rising again, until, at the outbreak of the war, *Tribunes* were being sent to nearly 300,000 subscribers of the daily, weekly, and semiweekly editions. The *Weekly*, as the *Tribune* liked to point out at this juncture, "is known . . . as the standard and favorite paper of common people; found in more village stores and offices, mechanics' workshops and farmers' homes than any other paper in the country." In contrast, the semiweekly, published Wednesday and Saturday, "circulates almost entirely among the educated and professional classes at points more or less remote from New York where local daily papers are depended upon for the telegraphic news." As if this were not enough, the *Tribune* also was publishing a special edition for European readers (issued on the departure of each mail steamer for Liverpool) and, finally, a post-Gold Rush edition for "California, Oregon and the Sandwich Islands" (published on the departure of each mail steamer for Aspinwell, the transshipment point on the Isthmus of Panama). Greeley could truly boast that his papers were seen each week by more than a million Americans.

And as the paper's influence and circulation grew, so did the influence and authority of its editor. Greeley's lectures, particularly in the West, were extremely popular, and his words, as embodied in *Tribune* editorials, were considered the final authority on almost every subject.*

In the slaveholding states, of course, Greeley's abolitionist dogma was anathema. Sam Houston called the editor a man "whose hair is white, whose skin is white, whose eyes are white, whose clothes are white, and whose liver is, in my opinion, of the same color." Nevertheless, the *Tribune* was carefully studied

During the Civil War the Tribune *made as well as reported news. Draft rioters attacked its offices, and correspondent Smalley's Antietam dispatches were Washington's first hard news of the battle. Some stories broke after press time, as the item at center indicates. Home base at the time was the Old Rookery on Nassau Street. There were always people waiting—and waiting—to see the editor.*

---

*It is ironic in this context that the quotation most often attributed to him, "Go West, young man," was not original with Greeley, but represented, rather, the advice of an Indiana editor, John Soule of the Terre Haute *Express*, and was always so attributed by Greeley.

in the South—if for no other reason than that its editorials were believed to represent the true voice of the North. Not that its editor was ever consistent on the question of how far opposition to slavery should be carried. First the *Tribune* categorically opposed its extension to the territories, then accepted the Missouri Compromise, then reverted to its original opposition. When southerners began talking about secession, Greeley appeared amenable. The right of secession, the *Tribune* said, "may be a revolutionary one. . . . It exists nevertheless." But then Greeley hedged that right with impossible conditions, and eventually he concluded that secession was "treason."

Leaders in the North found him equally hard to pin down. Instrumental in the nomination of Lincoln (turning his back on his former colleague in Congress, Seward, Greeley held fast with Edward Bates, a conservative, and this helped open the door for the Rail Splitter), the editor soon began chevying the new President. Asked once why he did not reply to a distorted *Tribune* story, Lincoln told an aide, "Yes, all the newspapers will publish my comment on it, and so will Greeley. The next day he will take a line and comment on it, and he will keep it up in that way, and at the end of three weeks I will be convicted out of my own mouth of all the things which he charges against me. No man, whether he be private citizen or President of the United States, can successfully carry on a controversy with a great newspaper and escape destruction unless he owns a newspaper equally great with a circulation in the same neighborhood."

So the *Tribune* ranted on unchecked, expressing Greeley's abomination of slavery, running morbid accounts of Negroes burned at the stake, of the hanging and torture of slaves, and dubious reports of the activities of a possibly fictional slave trader in New Orleans. The battle was waged even in local items:

"IN FEAR—The U.S. Marshal of Massachusetts has applied to the Marshal here for an escort for the fugitive Sims when he is passing through the city. Of course, he will get it. The Chief could not be hired to let such an opportunity to exhibit his new shooting iron escape. Yes, Mr. Massachusetts Negro-Catcher, you shall have safe passage for yourself and followers through the City of Gotham."

As secession approached, the *Tribune* appeared to be resigned to the possibility of war, and even to welcome it. "Let this intolerable suspense and uncertainty cease," it proclaimed on April 2, 1861. "The country, with scarcely a show of dissent, cries out—if we are to fight, so be it." And, on April 15, 1861, it trumpeted, "Fort Sumter is lost, but freedom is saved." The *Tribune* started in the war with a hawkish scowl, castigating Union generals, and the President too, for not marching across the Potomac and sweeping through the South. When the Confederate congress announced its intention to convene in Richmond, the daily *Tribune* ran above its editorial column, in standing italic type, the legend "Forward to Richmond! Forward to Richmond! The Rebel Congress must not be allowed to meet there on the 20th of July. By that date, the place must be held by the National Army." At least partly as a result of such pressure from the *Tribune*, and other papers as well, the Union armies did advance, and were brutally mauled on July 21 at Bull Run.

The reaction in the North was strong, and much of it was aimed at the *Tribune*. The man who was responsible for the headline found himself in a vulnerable position: on March 27, 1862, Dana was notified by the Tribune Association that Greeley had requested his resignation.

The next managing editor was Sydney Howard Gay, a man much more amenable to discipline than his predecessor. His term of office lasted only through the war, however; in 1866 he retired for reasons of health. But it was during Gay's administration that the *Tribune* did much of its best journalistic work. The paper's editorial page may have been subject to attack for its blatant misreading of facts (at first it called Bull Run a Union victory), but the news reporting remained straight—and

In Greeley's last years scandal hit the Tribune *when a reporter was killed by his paramour's jealous ex-husband. Staffers were still working where they could—baggage cars included—to score news beats. Heir apparent Whitelaw Reid (standing) took over when Greeley, stunned by his electoral defeat, died in 1872. By 1881, with funds from his wife's family fortune, Reid's control was secure.*

it remained good. Correspondent Albert D. Richardson managed to give *Tribune* readers the first uncensored, detailed account of Sumter's fall. Captured later in the war by the Rebels, he escaped from the Confederate penetentiary at Salisbury, North Carolina, and made his way to Knoxville, Tennessee, from where he wired the *Tribune*, "Out of the jaws of death. Out of the mouth of hell," and went back on the job. Probably the *Tribune*'s outstanding journalistic exploit of the war, however, was George W. Smalley's dispatch on the Battle of Antietam, which was intercepted by Union censors to provide President Lincoln with his first news of the battle. Smalley, rushing back to New York, still arrived in time to give the *Tribune* the first battle accounts.

Through its news pages, and particularly through the work of the twenty-odd correspondents Greeley assigned to the war, the *Tribune* was able to win back the prestige that its unwise editorials had cost it, and eventually President Lincoln was forced to take it into account. When Greeley, in a famous editorial, "The Prayer for 20 Million," urged upon the President the emancipation of all slaves in the freed territories, Lincoln put aside his scruples about making a reply to Greeley. A paragraph from his letter to the *Tribune* is generally cited as the true position of the Great Emancipator on the question of the Union and slavery:

"My primary object in this struggle is to save the Union, and is NOT either to save or destroy slavery. If I could save the Union without freeing ANY slaves, I would do it; and if I could save it by freeing ALL the slaves, I would do it, and if I could save it by freeing some and leaving others slaves, I would also do that."

The *Tribune* did not emerge from the war either physically or fiscally unscathed. The hostilities, as the *Tribune*

complained, occasioned "a sudden and rapid increase in the cost of our paper and other materials." The newsstand price leaped, in two jumps, to four cents, but still the *Tribune* lost money. Physically, however, the Great Moral Organ's staff and office remained strong enough to withstand attacks by murderous rioters who roared through New York City after the passage of the draft laws in July, 1863. The mob, which set fire to the Negro orphanage on Fifth Avenue above Forty-third Street and murdered dozens of Negroes of all ages, made two attacks on the *Tribune* itself, gaining entrance during one and setting several small fires. With the aid of a platoon of policemen, however, the rioters were driven from the office before any serious damage was done. During a lull in the furious four days, a correspondent from the Cincinnati *Gazette*, Whitelaw Reid, who was to become Greeley's final adjutant and his eventual successor, visited the *Tribune* and described the scene:

"Muskets were provided for every employee. The floor of the editorial room was littered with hand grenades, and extra bayonets were lying about on the desks like some new pattern of mammoth pen holders. Arrangements for pouring a volume of scalding steam into the lungs of anybody attempting to force an entrance had been perfected. In the midst of all the warlike preparations, Mr. Greeley, coat off and apparently just risen from preparing a leader, was listening to the statements of his reporters as to the progress of the mob, and making suggestions for perfecting the defenses of the office."

The steam, however, was not needed. The *Tribune* managed to weather the war without further physical damage—although its reputation was again tarnished when Greeley, eager for peace and a negotiated settlement, became caught up

in spurious Confederate maneuvers intended to weaken Northern determination for a victory.

Understandably, the *Tribune* greeted Appomattox with the largest type in its history and eight subheads:

"VIRGINIA!
Lee Surrenders!
The Rebellion Ended!
Official Correspondence
General Lee Desirous of 'Peace'
Manly and Patriotic Letter from
General Grant
The Rebel Leader Must Lay Down
His Arms
He Capitulates on General Grant's
Own Terms
The Officers to be Paroled
and Sent Home"

Like the rest of America, the *Tribune* was shocked and demoralized by the assassination of President Lincoln four days later. The lead news story, on the aftermath of the war, had already been locked into place. There was barely time to turn the rules and compose the headlines that told the then incomplete story:

"HIGHLY IMPORTANT!
The President Shot!
Secretary Seward Attacked"

President Lincoln was dead and the nation leaderless. The next seven years would find the *Tribune* valiantly attempting—in the face of a good deal of competition—to fill the void. Greeley, predictably, offered his support to President Johnson at first, but by May of 1866, also predictably, he had turned upon the new administration. When it was suggested that the *Tribune*'s opposition might be mollified by the appointment of its editor as Postmaster General, President Johnson demurred that Greeley ran "to goodness of heart so much as to produce infirmity of mind."

Perhaps the President had a point, for it was in this period that Greeley made his bravest, and most unpopular, decision—and he made it in full knowledge of the calamitous consequences that would descend both upon himself and upon the *Tribune*. Since the end of the war, the editor had called for leniency for the South. "Universal Amnesty and Impartial Suffrage" was the *Tribune*'s editorial slogan, and Greeley proved he meant what he said when on May 13, 1867, he joined a number of others in signing the $100,000 bail bond that released Jefferson Davis from prison. The storm of abuse from vengeful elements in the North extended all the way to his club. Summoned to a special meeting of the Union League to explain his action, Greeley refused to appear. "Understand, once for all," he said in an open letter published in the *Tribune*, "that I dare you and defy you. . . . So long as any man was seeking to overthrow our Government, he was my enemy; from the hour in which he laid down his arms, he was my formerly erring countryman. . . ." The Union League met without Greeley, and backed down. The editor retained his membership, and the New York *Tribune* rode out yet another storm of cancelled subscriptions.

In 1867 Greeley, not fully satisfied with his managing editor, John Russell Young, began making overtures to Whitelaw Reid, the Cincinnati correspondent who had impressed him with his coverage of the Civil War, and later of Washington. Earlier in the *Tribune*'s history Greeley had complained that "of all horned cattle, a college graduate in a newspaper office is the worst," but, having watched Reid's work, the editor was willing to overlook the fact that he was a graduate of Miami University at Oxford, Ohio. He was also willing to hint of a possible succession to the helm of the *Tribune*, and, as a result, early in the fall

Elizabeth Mills Reid

of 1868 Whitelaw Reid, at age thirty-five, accepted the position of "first writing editor" of the *Tribune*. The next spring Young resigned, and Greeley posted a notice that read: "The office of managing editor is abolished, and Mr. Whitelaw Reid will see that Mr. Greeley's orders are obeyed, and give instructions at any time in his absence to subordinates."

Reid quickly justified Greeley's expectations. He picked up the *Tribune* style at once, and readers were soon hard pressed to distinguish between his editorials and those of the master. And if Greeley was pleased with his new assistant, so was the staff. Although a hard man with a blue pencil, Reid had a policy of standing by his men when they were under attack: he also introduced at the *Tribune* a policy of expressing appreciation for staff members who had performed outstanding work. The expression often took the form of cash.

Greeley had thrown the paper wholeheartedly into the movement to impeach President Johnson, and Reid kept it in the forefront of that battle. He made a point of keeping ahead on other fronts as well. Smalley, the Civil War correspondent who had become the *Tribune*'s "foreign commissioner," was directed to "place no limitation upon your expenditures" in keeping the *Tribune* ahead in the coverage of the Franco-Prussian War. Cable tolls after the battles of Sedan and Gravelotte amounted to as much as $4,000 per day, but the complete beats scored by Smalley and other *Tribune* correspondents did much to bring the paper's circulation back out of the pit again.

Also contributing to the rejuvenation of the paper was the service done for the *Tribune* by the United States Senate, which in 1871 was shocked to find the text of a secret treaty it had been de-

bating spread all over the front page of the *Tribune*. The question of how the editors got the text eventually overshadowed the Senate debate altogether. "If the government can't keep its own secrets, we do not propose to undertake the contract," the *Tribune* said editorially, but the Senate was not inclined to let it go at that. The two *Tribune* correspondents in Washington, H. J. Ramsdell and Zebulon White, were asked to disclose their sources, and when they refused, the Senate voted to have them arrested and confined to the "apartments of the Pacific Railroad Committee." These, however, proved to be spacious and comfortable, and the two men, who received double pay during their arrest, found the ordeal far from unpleasant. White's dispatches, datelined "The Senate Bastille, U. S. Capitol," described in genial detail the furnishings of the well-appointed apartments, the meals brought for the prisoners from the Senate restaurant, and their conversations with a number of distinguished—and amused—visitors. After ten days, the reporters were, by vote of the Senate, released from their imprisonment.

There were other attractions for readers of the *Tribune* in these days. Reid dispatched his best friend, John Hay, who had been President Lincoln's private secretary and was to become Secretary of State under President Theodore Roosevelt, to Chicago to cover the fire that broke out Sunday, October 8, 1871. The *Tribune* got a first bulletin into its Monday edition under the heading, "Postscript 4 A.M.," and continued to front-page the fire dispatches until October 26.

Inside the paper, the columns were becoming more exciting, too. William Winter, considered America's greatest authority on acting, was beginning to upset theatregoers and performers with his drama reviews. On one occasion Winter wrote that a pair playing Romeo

and Juliet "resembled nothing so much as a pair of amorous grasshoppers pursuing their stridulous loves in the hollow of a cabbage leaf." And not all the romances in the *Tribune* were the subjects of theatre reviews. "We are happy to announce," the paper trumpeted in 1871, "we have commenced the publication of a local romance calculated to shake society to its center. It contains, indeed, more truth than fiction, for the mind of man has not yet conceived such horrors and atrocities as surround the hapless working girls of our great city. This great story is entitled Bertha, the Sewing Machine Girl; or, Death at the Wheel. . . ."

In city news the *Tribune* had much to choose from, although here it—and the rest of the town as well—had to follow in the tracks of the *New York Times*. Raymond had died in 1869, but his successor, George Jones, who had known Horace Greeley when the latter was a printer's devil on the East Poultney, Vermont, *Northern Spectator*, had taken out in full cry after the Democratic political boss, William Marcy Tweed. The *Times* got him, too, after a disgruntled Tammany adjutant, former Sheriff James O'Brien, turned over to it the records that eventually sent Tweed to the Tombs. The *Tribune*, quibbling jealously that the *Times* appeared to have obtained the evidence "in some surreptitious way," could only applaud the disclosures against its traditional enemy, the Democratic machine. The Great Moral Organ did, however, undertake an exposé of its own, centering its fire on another target of corruption, the customshouse; in November of 1871 it won a victory of sorts when Thomas Murphy, the port collector, resigned. Murphy's successor was, however, no more acceptable to Greeley and the *Tribune*. His name, incidentally, was Chester A. Arthur.

Greeley had other troubles with his city

Walt Whitman

Bret Harte

Harriet Beecher Sto.

Left: Mark Twain

staff. Despite all his teaching—and his example—not all his subordinates were hewing to the path of morality. In 1869, he had been forced to ask for the resignation of Amos J. Cummings, an excellent city editor (and the man credited with coining the man-bites-dog definition of news). Cummings, it was said, had persisted, despite several warnings, in swearing on the job. There was another, far more serious incident in the city room in 1869, when Albert Richardson, the Civil War correspondent who had made such a spectacular escape from Confederate prison, failed altogether to escape from an irate husband who traced him to Park Row and shot and mortally wounded him within the confines of the *Tribune* offices. Greeley defended the conduct of his man as best he could, whereupon Dana, now editor of the *Sun*, chuckled and sent a reporter over to the *Tribune* to ask his former boss if it was true that the *Tribune* was infested with supporters of free love. The *Sun* quoted Greeley's answer: "By God, (bringing his venerable fist upon the desk) there is no such crowd, at least not around the *Tribune* office. The whole thing has been got up by the enemies of the *Tribune*." Greeley wrote a letter to the *Sun* to express his dissatisfaction with the published interview. He had not, he insisted, used the name of the Supreme Being.

The editor was nearing sixty by this time. Dispirited by the deaths of seven of his nine children, his strength sapped from overwork—he had continued to traverse the lecture circuit, and had, in addition, published six volumes of history, letters, and essays between 1863 and 1871—Greeley had grown sallow and paunchy. He still retained the white fringe of beard as well as some of the white hair which had become his trade-

mark, but recurring bouts of the malaria he had contracted on a visit to Nassau in 1870 left him visibly weakened. Yet Horace Greeley had one more hand to play. In 1872, the pioneer Republican ran for the Presidency—with the backing of the Democratic party.

This, of course, was the ultimate inconsistency, and Greeley was not without misgivings when he undertook his final battle against the political machine that had been running in well-oiled grooves during the first term of Ulysses S. Grant. In particular, he was worried about the effect his campaign would have on the *Tribune*, "of which so little is my own property that I dread to wreck it. . . ." Still, he went ahead. In May of 1872 the maverick Liberal Republican party nominated him for the Presidency; two months later the Democrats added their endorsement.

The campaign was, as Greeley must have known it would be, bitter and terrible. He resigned from the *Tribune* in May, and Reid took up the battle against the calumny that poured in from the regular-Republican papers. Greeley was linked, in editorial and cartoon, with free love, Boss Tweed, and the Ku Klux Klan. Possibly the unkindest cut came from the *Times*, which reported a Greeley meeting in Missouri at which a Confederate flag was hoisted "to create the necessary enthusiasm." The *Tribune* fought back, uncovering fresh scandals with which to assail Grant—but the effort was foredoomed. Not all the *Tribunes* even got to those subscribers who remained loyal: there were charges that Republican postmasters were substituting the *Times*.

The agony of the campaign was cruelly intensified for Greeley by the terminal illness of his wife of thirty-five years. For the month before the election, he was held close to the deathbed of Molly Greeley, who died October 30, just five days before her husband was swept to igno-

Before the Atlantic cable, competing newspapers sent dispatch boats to pick up foreign news from incoming steamers. Later, under Reid, the Tribune *got a fine new building, the "Tall Tower," and great contributors continued to use the paper as a showcase. John Hay, who later became Secretary of State under McKinley and T. R., was an able interim editor during Reid's extended wedding trip of 1881.*

minious defeat at the polls. Greeley carried only six states, and his total popular vote was disappointing, 2,834,079. Grant polled a plurality of more than three quarters of a million, a margin that stood as a record until 1900.

On November 7, 1872, Horace Greeley, weakened in health and spirit and impoverished in purse (he now owned only six shares of *Tribune* stock), attempted to pick up the threads. But it was no good. The editor was not himself, and before long, Reid was forced to step in and suppress an editorial in which Greeley attacked a previous—and lighthearted—editorial squib directed not at him but rather at the office seekers who had crowded around him. To have allowed Greeley to print his vicious and uncalled-for response, Reid said, "would have sent every editor out of the staff." The younger man prevailed, the card was suppressed, and, within a few days, Greeley returned to his home at Chappaqua, in suburban Westchester County. He died at the house of a nearby physician two weeks later, on November 29, 1872.

They may all have fought against him at various points of his life, but his contemporaries put on quite a funeral for Horace Greeley. The dignitaries, politicians, journalists, and officeholders whom the old editor had, by turns, supported and denounced, attended almost in a body. President Grant was there, of course, along with his Vice President-elect, Henry Wilson, and the outgoing Vice President, Greeley's old friend Schuyler Colfax. In the funeral procession, members of the Union League marched with members of Typographical Union Number Six, which says a lot about Horace Greeley.

The founder was gone, but the *Tribune*, to the surprise of many subscribers, still stood. Its shares were no longer worth the $10,000 they had commanded a few years before, but they did have value—particularly since a contest was looming for control. Whitelaw Reid was the heir apparent, of course, but Reid was, by his own estimation, "about the best hated man in New York." Greeley's campaign for the Presidency had cost the *Tribune* heavily among its Republican supporters, and Reid fell heir to that loss, as well as to the calumny that resulted when Dana at the *Sun* caught wind of the suppressed Greeley editorial. Reid, it

John Hay

was said, had broken the old man's heart, and this materially affected the new editor's standing among the members of the Tribune Association. But finally, with the help of Rhode Island's Senator William Sprague and Jay Gould, the financier, Reid managed to raise $500,000, and on December 23, 1872, he announced his purchase of a clear majority of the stock: "The associates and disciples of Horace Greeley, sensible of their inability to fill his place, strengthened by his teachings, and encouraged by his example, take up the burden of his life. . . ."

Among the rejoicers was *Tribune* correspondent Mark Twain. "The Lord knows I grieved to see the old *Tribune* wavering and ready to tumble into the common slough of journalism," he wrote Reid, "and God knows I am truly glad you saved it. I hope you will stand at its helm a hundred years."

Reid had his paper now—as well as an annual deficit that ran as high as $96,000. The *Weekly Tribune* was down from 200,000 subscribers to 150,000; the daily was running about 45,000—about equal to the *Herald*, and well behind the *Sun* at 100,000 and the *Times* at 50,000. At least part of the problem, Reid felt, was prestige. The *Tribune* had long since outgrown the five-story building at Spruce and Nassau streets, and the editor determined to replace it on the same site with the finest newspaper plant in New York. On April 10, 1875, the *Tribune*'s thirty-fourth anniversary, the paper was issued from its new one-million-dollar home. The nine-story building, with its 260-foot tower, was topped on the city's skyline only by the spire of Trinity Church. From the rotary perfecting press in the basement, which could turn out 16,000 papers every hour, all the way to the top floor, where there were stands for one hundred compositors, the new plant bespoke its editor's confidence.

The eighth-floor city room, with its map-covered walls, was described by an anonymous historian in the centennial edition of the *Herald Tribune* in 1941:

"There was a perpendicular viaduct for communication with the counting, editorial and composing rooms, with speaking tubes, copy boxes and bells. A water pail and a tin jar of ice water sat in a corner of the room. Paste pots and ink stands were scattered about, bits of blotting paper and rusty steel pens were on the floor. A dozen reporters sat at small green desks, some writing, some reading—several smoking briarwood pipes. Thatcher, the weather man, sat in a corner deciding it would rain within forty hours. Thatcher also ran a telescope business on the side (see the moon for a dime) in front of St. Paul's Church. Unoccupied reporters grumbled at the hours, which were usually noon to midnight, six days a week. . . ."

Well, if the reporters grumbled at the hours—which were standard—at least they had a powerful consolation. Next to the basement pressroom Reid had set up an employee tavern. A beer saloon was housed in the Great Moral Organ, and Horace Greeley not dead three years!

The saloon wasn't the only thing that would have upset Greeley. Two years and two pay cuts after they came to work in the "Tall Tower," eighty-nine members of the printers' union Greeley had helped found went out on strike. The cause, in addition to the twenty per cent cut in wages, was Reid's determination to eliminate from the contract the requirement that all matter set for the paper outside the shop be reproduced by *Tribune* printers. Ironically, this provision was also to be one of the sticking points in the labor disputes which, eighty-nine years later, led to the death of the *Herald Tribune;* but, for the present at least, Reid's financial returns were excellent. The *Tribune* brought in nonunion printers, weathered the financial panic that began in 1873, and by 1877 was even able to report an $85,000 profit.

Journalistically, too, the paper's reputation was improving, despite such unfortunate lapses as declaring Democrat Samuel Tilden the winner in the hotly contested presidential election of 1876. The *Tribune* more than made up for this, however, in 1878, when after months of work it deciphered and printed the "cipher dispatches," coded telegrams that showed that Tilden's campaign managers had been negotiating for the purchase of electoral votes in the South and West. The exposure—and proof—of this attempt to buy a presidential election is generally considered the best story of the *Tribune*'s 125-year career. And the paper's reputation for excellent writing was growing too. Work came in from, among others, Twain, Bret Harte, Walt Whitman, the noted English novelist Charles Reade, Harriet Beecher Stowe, and novelist Rebecca Harding Davis—mother of Richard Harding Davis, who was to be *the* journalist of the next generation, and of Charles Belmont Davis, who was to become the *Tribune*'s drama editor. In 1875 John Hay, no longer with the paper, recommended Henry James, who, he reported, "considers The Tribune the only paper where business could be combined with literary ambition." Nineteen of James's letters from Paris were published, but, as the novelist himself soon found, he was "too finical a writer" for newspapers, and he wrote no more for them.

The *Tribune* was also helped by Reid's decision to resume publication of the Sunday paper that Greeley had attempted in 1861 and then abandoned under pressure from the New York Sabbath Committee. Now, however, as Reid pointed out, "with the single exception of some of the clergy," all the defenders of the Sabbath "who were exhorting me to continue setting a noble example were gratifying their own craving to know what was going on by reading some Sunday paper." The sixteen-page Sunday *Tribune* first appeared on December 6, 1879, with departmental features that included Home Interests, Music, Studio and Gallery, Book Reviews, Knitting, Science for the People, and Religious Intelligence. It was, at least, a gentler Sunday paper than the *Herald* or the *Times*.

The **Tribune** *guessed wrong about the outcome of the election of 1876, but right about the Linotype: Reid (standing) backed Mergenthaler's revolutionary machine. Staff writers paused for a picture, the pressroom hummed, and crowds caught outdoor news bulletins. Whitelaw Reid's family—his son Ogden, Ogden's wife Helen, and grandsons Whitelaw II and Ogden—carried on the* Tribune.

TILDEN ELECTED.

HIS ELECTORAL MAJORITY SMALL.

HAYES AND WHEELER HAVE ABOUT 150 ELECTORAL VOTES—THE U. S. SENATE WILL HAVE A REDUCED REPUBLICAN MAJORITY—THE HOUSE IS CLOSE, WITH A PROBABLE SMALL DEMOCRATIC MAJORITY.

Tilden and Hendricks seem to be elected by a fair majority of the Electoral College. They have probably carried the "solid South" with the possible exception of South Carolina and Louisiana, have carried New-York by from 25,000 to 30,000 majority, Connecticut by about 1,500 majority, and New-Jersey by a reduced majority. They have carried Indiana by 10,000 majority. Their total vote in the Electoral College is likely to exceed 200. Hayes and Wheeler have carried all the New-England States except Connecticut, Pennsylvania, and all the Western States except Missouri. Their vote in the Electoral College will not fall much below 150.

Circulation, which stabilized at about 50,000 daily, 100,000 weekly, and 50,000 to 75,000 on Sunday, attracted enough advertising to enable Reid to double the Tribune Association capitalization and to pay off all but a small portion of the mortgage on the new building. In 1882, Reid ordered the addition of a twenty-story, steel-framed rear wing, thus doubling the building's rentable space. In his new and expensive ventures, the editor was aided by a new source of capital. He had married Miss Elizabeth Mills, the daughter of financier Darius Ogden Mills, in 1881, and Mills had picked up the *Tribune* shares owned by Jay Gould and given them to his son-in-law. Of the 200 shares, Reid now had 143, and was secure enough to dabble in philanthropy in his own right. The *Tribune* had taken over from the *Evening Post* the Fresh Air Fund, a charity devoted to providing rural summer vacations for slum children, and by 1888 more than ten thousand youngsters had benefited.

The good fortunes of the editor did not, however, extend to politics. In 1880, the *Tribune* had worked for the election of James A. Garfield, but only six months later an assassin's bullet promoted the paper's old target, Chester A. Arthur, to the Presidency. The *Tribune*'s choice in 1884 was Maine's James G. Blaine, who had considerable opposition among liberal Republicans. In the end, however, two of Blaine's friends cost him the election. One was a spokesman for a clerical delegation, who hailed the Republican as America's defender against "Rum, Romanism, and Rebellion" and thereby delivered the Roman Catholic vote to Grover Cleveland. Blaine's other friend and handicap was the New York *Tribune*.

The year before, while Reid was vacationing in Ohio, the strikebreakers he had hired in 1877 went over in a body to Typographical Union Number Six, which thereupon sought the discharge of the *Tribune*'s foreman, William P. Thompson, who was accused, among other things, of being an unreconstructed Rebel and of beating his wife. Reid returned from his vacation and hired more strikebreakers, and Typographical Union Number Six organized a boycott against "the most pronounced opponent of the working man in America, the New York *Tribune*." The resulting furor, as historian James G. Smart wrote in the *Nation*, was "so protracted and filled with such hatred that the rancor caused by it would take a long time in dying. Perhaps it never died."

"Boycott the *Tribune* and James G. Blaine" was the message of the printers' newspaper, the *Boycotter*, to the union's 3,500 members and 75,000 supporters. Blaine lost New York state by only 1,200 votes, and the Presidency by the margin of New York state's electoral votes.

The election of Grover Cleveland was not the only important result of the feud between the *Tribune* and its printers. It shares that distinction with the revolution caused in the industry when, in late 1885, Reid gave the freedom of his composing room to a Baltimore inventor named Ottmar Mergenthaler. Early in the morning of July 3, 1886, the *Tribune*'s nonunion printers were called to assemble around a heavy, squat piece of machinery on the ninth floor composing room. As Mergenthaler explained his project, Whitelaw Reid fingered the keys of the as yet unnamed device, and within seconds a small lead slug fell into a slot. Legend has it that Reid, at that moment, named the Linotype.

Automated typesetting, at three times the speed of hand printing, materially aided the *Tribune*'s fortunes; there was—for the moment—no union to protest its adoption, as a later union would protest later technological advances, with results painful for the newspaper. The Linotype also aided the fortunes of Reid, who be-

came the treasurer of the syndicate formed to underwrite it. As both the *Tribune* and his new enterprise prospered, the editor turned more and more toward public service.

In the election of 1888, Reid supported Benjamin Harrison and as a result was considered the likely choice for ambassador to the Court of St. James's. The *Tribune*'s stand in favor of Irish home rule militated against that, however, and the editor was persuaded by his old friend Blaine, now Secretary of State, to accept the second-ranking diplomatic job, the ambassadorship to France. He was abroad three years—returning briefly in 1891 for the fiftieth-anniversary celebration of the *Tribune* at the Metropolitan Opera House. The featured speaker on that occasion was, of all people, Charles Dana, who mused that "the world has changed. . . . It is wonderful how little personal controversy there is in our great newspapers."

Reid's absence from the turbulence of domestic politics helped to heal a number of other wounds, and on his return for the Republican convention of 1892 he found himself a principal candidate for the Vice Presidency under Harrison. There was, however, enough opposition to persuade the Ambassador to stop in New York and make peace with Typographical Union Number Six. Reid went to the convention in Milwaukee with a signed statement from the printers that "the *Tribune* is now a strict union office." He was nominated for Vice President by acclamation, but the ticket of Harrison and Reid went down to defeat by 363,612 votes before the comeback of Grover Cleveland.

Disappointed, Reid returned to the *Tribune*, but his heart really wasn't in it. Joseph Pulitzer was well on the way to revolutionizing New York journalism, but the man now considered "the dean

of the press in New York" seemed to have lost interest in the dirty little wars of newspapers. He was away much of the time, lecturing at Yale, travelling to Europe, vacationing in the Adirondacks, or resting at the western estates of his father-in-law. A supporter of McKinley, of course, he was named in 1898 to the commission that met in Paris to draft the peace treaty with Spain, and in 1902 President Theodore Roosevelt sent Reid as his representative at the coronation of Edward VII. Four years later, T. R. named him to the post for which he had long been considered, ambassador to the Court of St. James's. John Hay, by now Secretary of State, said that signing Reid's commission was "the crowning act of friendship and close association of forty years."

While Reid was climbing to the apex of his diplomatic career, the *Tribune* was beginning to plunge toward its nadir. Reid, too good a newsman not to have seen it coming, spoke as early as 1879 of the opportunity awaiting the publisher of a paper that would be "as disreputable and vile as 150,000 readers would be willing to buy." In 1883, Pulitzer seized the opportunity by buying the *World*, and four years later, William Randolph Hearst came along to buy control of the *Journal*. These press lords jumped onto —indeed, Hearst helped propel—the Spanish-American War bandwagon. The *World* and *Journal* paid $2.12 per word cable costs for news from Cuba, and their editors called for bigger and bigger sizes of railroad type to display it, but the *Tribune*, for the most part, relied on the Associated Press and featured local stories. At least part of the problem was that Reid, in his absences from the paper, had placed in charge men of long service who were, as Harry W. Baehr, Jr., points out in his *The New York Tribune Since the Civil War*, "not the type to alter fixed modes of thought and action on the paper."

Indeed, Reid's regents had all they could do to convince Reid to adopt two-column headlines, and to follow the trend toward Sunday magazines and daily sports pages. They could not, however, persuade him to meet the price competition of the yellow press. Both the *World* and the *Journal* were selling at one cent a copy. Only grudgingly had Reid cut the *Tribune*'s price from four to three cents; further he would not go. But in 1898 Adolph S. Ochs, who had purchased the critically weak *New York Times* two years before, put his paper before his pride. He took the *Times* down to a penny to challenge the *World* and the *Journal*, and he made a success of it. The *Times* tripled its circulation and soared past the *Tribune*. For eleven more years, while Reid railed at the "penny press" and clung to the concept of a newspaper edited "for the gentry," the *Tribune* sold for three cents and lost about a million dollars each year. When the editor finally yielded, in 1909, he was too late. Horace Greeley's *Tribune*, "the bible of the West" had become known as "the little old lady of Park Row."

Whitelaw Reid died at his post in England in 1912 and was succeeded in control of the *Tribune* by his son Ogden, a Yale Law School graduate who had been trained successively as reporter, city editor, and managing editor. Ogden Reid needed money to build, and he got it from his mother—several million dollars in advances. These and earlier family loans to the paper were covered by notes that would play a major role in the death of the paper, but for the present they gave young Reid a chance to breathe. The by-lines and the forthcoming display of the work of men such as Heywood Broun, W. O. McGeehan, Franklin Pierce Adams, and Grantland Rice soon indicated the new direction the *Tribune*'s third master was taking. If it

couldn't match its competitors in covering the news, the *Tribune* would take the alternative course: it would write its way to success.

Yet of all the *Tribune* writers—many of whom became well known, and some even famous—few promoted the fortunes of the paper so well as a thirteen-year-old Brooklyn girl. If the New York *Sun* is remembered as the paper Virginia wrote to about Santa Claus, then the *Tribune* deserves a place in history for the 1916 letter of Marjorie Sterrett:

"To the Editor of the New York Tribune, Dear Sir:—

I read in your paper every morning a lot about preparedness. My Grandpa and my great Grandpa were soldiers. If I was a boy I would be a soldier, too, but I am not, so I want to do what I can to help. Mama gives me a dime every week for helping her. I am sending you this week's dime to help build a battleship for Uncle Sam. I know a lot of other kids who would give their errand money if you would start a fund. I am thirteen years old, and go to Public School No. 9, Brooklyn.

Very truly yours,
Marjorie Sterrett

I am a true blue American and I want to see Uncle Sam prepared to lick all creation like John Paul Jones did.
P.S.—Please call the battleship *America*."

Marjorie never got her battleship—the exigencies of the military situation just did not call for one at the time—but the Battleship *America* Fund did win both prestige and circulation for the *Tribune*. Nevertheless, the increasing receipts did not enable Reid to match, in the years following World War I, the solid economic foundations that Ochs and his heirs, the Sulzbergers, were building to support the news-gathering expenditures of the New York *Times*. And while the *Times* poured its profits back

Stanley Walker   *George S. Kaufman*

Franklin P. Adams

into development, the Reids were finding it a struggle merely to approximate their competitor's daily news operations. Ogden Reid was not unwilling to invest a share of the *Tribune*'s profits; there were simply no profits to invest. In 1922 his brilliant wife, Helen Rogers Reid, who had taken over the business management of the paper, threw a banquet for its executives. "It's been a glorious year," she announced. "We only lost $150,000."

During the twenties, the paper made great progress with department-store advertising, which Helen Reid, an ex-suffragette, went after aggressively. With this new momentum, money was borrowed to erect a plant on Fortieth Street, between Seventh and Eighth avenues. And in 1924, five million dollars more went to purchase the competing New York *Herald*. Remembered primarily as the paper that had sent Stanley to find Livingstone, the *Herald* and its father-and-son publishers, James Gordon Bennett, Senior and Junior, had made a number of contributions to the newspaper business. The paper virtually discovered Wall Street, and it led in financial news. It was also the first paper to give serious coverage of crime news, and before falling into the hands of newspaper entrepreneur Frank Munsey in 1920, it was unexcelled in foreign coverage. Munsey soon came to the conclusion that his newest property and the *Tribune* were knocking each other out in competition for the same readers. "Do you buy us, or do we buy you?" he asked the Reids. "We buy you," Whitelaw Reid's widow replied. The *Tribune*, it was explained to the surprised Munsey, was a family obligation and, as such, not for sale. "I had no such obligation," Munsey said later. "So I sold to them." And while he was about it, he threw into the bargain the younger Bennett's Paris *Herald*.

Three of Munsey's assets were brought into the new Fortieth Street building: the name of the *Herald*; a young reporter, soon promoted to city editor, named Stanley Walker; and the bulk of the *Herald*'s circulation. Before the merger, the *Herald* had 175,000 and the *Tribune* 140,000 readers. The *Herald Tribune* came up with more than 275,000 which, while still less than the *Times*, provided the cushion that carried the paper up to World War II. Thus began what A. J. Liebling described in *The New Yorker* as the Silver Age of the *Herald Tribune*—"so called because of its gently elegiac quality and because a man on the paper could carry away his pay in quarters without making a bulge in his pants pocket."

Unionized printers were making more than fifty dollars a week by now, but writers were willing to work for less than twenty under city-desk giants like Walker and a successor, L. L. Engelking. In 1959, Walker, in a reminiscent mood, listed in the *Saturday Review* some of the more notable *Tribune* writers: "Alva Johnston, Ed Angly, Joe Driscoll and Ishbel Ross . . . Joseph Alsop, Sanderson Vanderbilt, Tom Sugrue, Ben Robertson, St. Clair McKelway, Tom Waring, John O'Reilly, Homer Bigart, John Lardner, Jack Gould, James T. Flexner, Lincoln Barnett, Bruce Pinter, Maron Simon, Beverly Smith, Joseph Mitchell and Joel Sayre. . . . What a brilliant, gallant troop of journalistic cavalrymen!"

Some names are missing here, like Walter Millis and Irita Van Doren, but cavalrymen wasn't a bad way of putting it. Most came to the *Herald Tribune*, lived in genteel poverty long enough to make their reputations, and rode off again to better-paying jobs on other papers and on magazines. Fortunately, the supply of ambitious apprentices was inexhaustible. "It was these eager, intelligent and unterrified youngsters," Walker wrote, "who gave the paper its distinctive flavor, a flavor which made it readable to a literate Tammany boss, a college president, and the more brainy taxicab drivers."

Most of the writing was excellent, but ironically the *Herald Tribune* story most often recalled by newspapermen is one from 1924 that turned out not to be true. For five days, before admitting it had been hoaxed, the paper headlined the reports of Sanford Jarrell, who stood Prohibition New York on its ear with bulletins about the activities, appointments, and patrons of a mysterious floating nightclub which, alas, turned out to exist nowhere but in his imagination.

The attraction of the *Herald Tribune* for writers continued to grow, and so did its camaraderie. Downstairs, behind what was coming to be known as the "newspaperman's newspaper" ("I shivered when they called it that," George Cornish, Reid's longtime editor, recently recalled. "Newspapermen's newspapers always seem to fold."), was Jack Bleeck's, the newspaperman's saloon. It did a great business with the staff. ("Drink is the curse of the *Tribune*," the epigram went, "and sex the bane of the *Times*.")

While Ogden Reid was democratically rubbing elbows at Bleeck's with columnist Lucius Beebe and the members of a fellowship later dubbed by John Lardner "the West Fortieth Street Browning Society," the *Herald Tribune* was expanding into the lower floors of a twenty-two-story building constructed on a plot to the rear of the main building. But internally the depression of the early thirties brought financial difficulties for the management. Just before her death in 1931, Mrs. Whitelaw Reid made available more family credit, to the tune of $400,000, to help tide the paper over.

Debt hung over the *Herald Tribune*, and its main rival, the *Times*, had an unshakable hold on certain revenue-producing groups of readers—the "classified" readers (some 75,000); the obituary followers; and garment executives, whose activities the *Times* had covered for fifty years. During the late thirties and the war years, the *Herald Tribune* held its own in circulation and gained very slightly in its share of the total advertising in New York newspapers. The advance of Allied armies in Europe enabled the Reids to reopen the European edition of the *Herald Tribune* in Paris, in December, 1944. It

In the **Tribune's Silver Age**, *during the twenties, Stanley Walker was its crack city editor. Messrs. Kaufman, Adams, and Beebe brightened its pages; Walter Lippmann's column was advertised on horse-drawn delivery wagons; Robert Benchley was a reporter. Newspapers were still laboriously sorted and folded by hand—and, except for personnel, the city room scene had not changed much either.*

Robert Benchley
Left: Lucius Beebe

proved immediately and unexpectedly profitable. Unlike the prewar paper, it looked almost the twin of its parent—the same eight-column pages, the same Bodoni heads, many of the same features.

The Paris edition, of course, was thin, and people who had enjoyed its handy readability would sometimes return to New York and suggest to the Reids that the parent paper would be better that way too, without all that clutter of advertising. Subscribers to the Paris edition actually paid more of the cost of their newspaper. Back in New York, perhaps in that spirit, Ogden Reid raised the price of the daily and Sunday editions on January 1, 1947, just three days before his unexpected death. If the *Times* went along, fine, he told his subordinates, and if it didn't, "I think the paper is strong enough to stand it." The evening papers also raised prices, but the *Times* matched only the Sunday increase, from ten to fifteen cents, and for nearly three years the flourishing daily *Times* undersold the daily *Herald Tribune*. This inevitably took some toll of readers. "Nobody in New York is going to pay a nickel for the *Herald Tribune* when they can get the *Times* for three cents," the general manager of the *Times*, Julius Adler, is said to have remarked at a meeting of newspaper executives during that period. "That's the way to put a competitor out of business."

For a good many years before the death of her husband, and as his health declined, Helen Reid had increasingly taken over the management of the newspaper. She supervised the advertising sales, ran the famous Forums, kept closely in touch with Irita Van Doren's book section, and helped found and operate *This Week*, long the *Herald Tribune*'s magazine section. She had the contacts with public figures, she saw the Presidents, she was on the firing line all day. After watching Dorothy Thompson and her in action, Winston Churchill once observed to young Whitelaw, Helen's eldest son, that perhaps all newspapers ought to be run by women.

After the war, Mrs. Reid turned the editorial side over to quiet, reserved Whitelaw. It was soon noticed that the *Tribune* under him was taking on and publishing a great many of his fellows from the class of 1936 at Yale—among them Stewart Alsop, who came in to work with his columnist brother, Joseph;

John Crosby, a columnist on radio and television; and August Heckscher (today New York's parks commissioner), chief editorial writer.

In the late forties, the *Herald Tribune* was still earning its way, but its financial difficulties were mounting. Costs rose until the annual increase, in the early 1950's, was a million dollars. The staff, overloaded with wartime returnees, was gradually pared by about ten per cent, but not without an outcry. The story goes that the paper's famous sports editor, Stanley Woodward, who had been responsible for bringing the *Herald Tribune* Red Smith, its unrivalled sports columnist, was asked which two men his department could spare. "Red Smith and me," Woodward said. In fact, Smith stayed, but Woodward left not long afterward. News coverage was cut back, at least in comparison with the vast news-gathering machinery of the *Times*. But paradoxically, even as its reputation in this department waned, its political power seemed to wax. As the *Tribune*'s endorsement had assuredly helped Wendell Willkie to the presidential nomination in 1940, eleven years later the paper launched Dwight Eisenhower to the Presidency with a two-column page-one editorial.

Now the paper was first in the White House, but far from that on New York newsstands. Whitelaw Reid tried to attract readers with various editorial devices—roving teams of writers to compensate in part for the reduced foreign bureaus, new columnists from Billy Rose to Art Buchwald. He brought in Walter Kerr as drama critic, Roscoe Drummond, and the cartoons of Bill Mauldin. An "early bird" edition was brought out at 7:30 P.M., but it failed to win away very much business from the afternoon papers.

In the early days of young Whitelaw's

editorship, during the late forties, the Reids had more to worry them than costs and prices. The new management was liberal in its Republicanism and was sometimes known to readers of columnist Westbrook Pegler (and later to McCarthy supporters) as the "Uptown *Daily Worker*," a rather astonishing view but one that sometimes hurt. Worse than that, a source of anxiety, damaging rumor, and great financial drain, was the debt incurred before the First World War—the moneys that the elder Reids had advanced to the paper. The old *Tribune* had given notes for this money, and on Mrs. Whitelaw Reid's death the notes had been divided, with a face value of three million each, between her son Ogden and his sister Jean, the wife of Sir John Ward, a former royal equerry. While Ogden never attempted to collect on the notes and further indebtedness due him, and turned it all over to the Reid Foundation, Lady Ward's lawyers began to press for payment when the first of her notes fell due, for $150,000, on April 15, 1948. It was paid. The next annual payment, for the same amount, could not be met in full, and was not entirely retired until 1952, by which time, of course, much more debt had accrued. A third of the $150,000 due for 1950 was paid off by 1954, and thereafter Lady Ward saw no more money.

In these circumstances, with a family debt that took precedence over payments on the *Tribune*'s mortgage, reorganization was clearly called for. Those who held the debts were in the driver's seat, and they elected in 1955 to turn the paper over to young Whitelaw's aggressive and dynamic younger brother, Odgen R. "Brown" Reid. Whitelaw, who had briefly replaced his mother as president, was elevated to the honorary position of chairman of the board. Helen Reid was in effect retired, and the noteholders got stock for what was owed

Bright sunset: The Herald Tribune *of the 1940's and 50's had its complement of top journalists, many of whom are still active. Backing them up were people like Eve Peterson (second from left), highly competent longtime secretary to* Tribune *brass. Many of its overseas bureaus closed, but the* Tribune *retained an international readership that apparently included at least one Egyptian camel driver.*

WORLD JOURNAL TRIBUNE

Walter Millis

them. As stock, it was, of course, subordinate to the mortgage, an arrangement that alone made possible the refinancing that kept Brown Reid in power for a few twilight years.

As editor, Brown Reid tinkered frequently with the *Herald Tribune*'s outward aspects. The sports section was printed on mint-green paper, and the paper's traditional makeup was "brightened." His most successful contribution was a revamping of the Sunday paper, which was slipping toward what was felt to be a point of no return: a circulation of less than half a million. Among the innovations was a small television program guide which, while never an advertising success in itself, did reverse the downward circulation trend. The Sunday paper went from 528,000 in 1954 to 576,000 in 1956.

The gentle Republican liberalism of the younger Whitelaw's regime seemed to turn to the right in the McCarthy era, and in some other respects the new editor rouged up the "little old lady of Park Row" into a trollop. Crime and divorce stories began getting prominent play, and publicity pictures of starlets were splashed through the news sections.

Not all staff members were in accord. Two-time Pulitzer prize winner Homer Bigart, back from Korea, shook his head and went to the *Times*. Other resignations came from Washington Bureau Chief Walter Kerr (not the drama critic) and City Editor Fendall Yerxa. Unquestionably, the "new image" attracted readers, but to the Reids' dismay every convert appeared to be matched by a defector from the ranks of the stolid, suburban, well-to-do readership of the "old" *Herald Tribune*.

None of Brown's devices availed to hold back the rising costs or augment the diminishing revenues. Brown Reid faced a difficult decision—whether to gamble on another price rise or to seek support outside the family. In 1957, he chose the latter, turning to a man with whom Whitelaw and others in the management had already held preliminary discussions. This was John Hay Whitney, at the time President Eisenhower's ambassador to the Court of St. James's.

Whitney was eligible on three counts. He had the money; he was a strong supporter of the liberal wing of the Republican party; and, as important as these other reasons, he was the grandson of John Hay, who had been the elder Whitelaw Reid's best friend, editorial writer, and, during Reid's honeymoon in 1881, substitute editor of the *Tribune*. The Ambassador first lent the Reids $1.2 million secured by stock options, and a year later, on August 28, 1958, in exchange for an additional sum reported by *Fortune* as two million dollars, he exercised his options and became possessed of the assets, good will, and current obligations of the New York *Herald Tribune*.

Editorially, Whitney used his new property with courage and dexterity. In 1964, for the first time since Horace Greeley, the *Tribune* endorsed a Democratic presidential nominee; and even in its dying days the paper played a considerable role in making possible the nomination and election of a liberal Republican, John V. Lindsay, as mayor of New York City.

What Whitney did not do, however, was fulfill the promise that his money would, as Joseph Kraft had predicted in *Harper's*, "cast the long shadow of a circulation war over the country's most competitive market." Alas, it was not to be. Whitney chose the businesslike way. Even before selecting his first editor, Robert M. White, the forty-four-year-old editor and publisher of the Mexico, Missouri, *Ledger*, Whitney ordered a detailed management survey of the *Herald Tribune*.

The recommendations that subsequently greeted White in New York involved nothing more than the same old editorial sleight of hand that the Reid family had been trying without success to pull off for nearly sixty years. Costs—particularly the cost of newsprint—would have to be cut. Condense the news and don't cover as much of it, the analysts said. Rely more heavily on the wire services. Already the deficiencies in *Herald Tribune* reporting were all too apparent to the readers. Now, even on local stories, the staff was to "interpret" whatever came across the Associated Press and United Press International teletypes, reporting that is primarily geared to radio and television stations and small papers interested in skimming off the top of the news.

As editor, however, White made his reputation by ignoring not only the management recommendations but, unfortunately, many of the editorial news conferences as well. He tinkered a little with the makeup, but the improvement failed to provide the dramatic impact Whitney was seeking, and White's departure was insured by the *Herald Tribune*'s reporting of the 1960 election. (The paper seems to have been a perennial bad guesser on national elections. In 1876 it had given the victory to Tilden over Hayes, and in 1916, when Charles Evans Hughes went to bed early thinking he had been elected, so did the *Tribune*. A young reporter named Robert Benchley learned that California had unexpectedly put Woodrow Wilson back into office, but when he called the city desk at 3 A.M., nobody answered.) In 1960, the *Herald Tribune* went to press early again, proclaiming a Kennedy victory of "Rooseveltian proportions." The extremely close returns, accurately reported by the *Times*, resulted in embarrassment for Whitney. He came back from London, and White went back to Mexico, Missouri.

For his next editor, Whitney didn't

eph Alsop

Art Buchwald

Red Smith

Homer Bigart

John Crosby

reach so far—only across town to hire away John Denson, the editor of *Newsweek*. Whitney wanted an impact, and Denson set out to give him one. First and foremost he fiddled with the headlines. No longer were these to be mere summaries of stories. Henceforth they would reflect the *significance* of the news. Dashes, colons, and question marks—lots of question marks—sprang into the headlines. The Bay of Pigs crisis in March, 1961, a month after his arrival, gave Denson a chance to show what he was up to. "DICTATOR CASTRO—THE BEGINNING OF THE END?" the *Herald Tribune* headed the first report. "SOVIETS WILL OPPOSE US ON CUBA—BUT HOW?" it asked next. Then: "ANTI-CASTRO RAIDERS IN TROUBLE?" And finally: "IT'S A GAME—WHO TAKES THE BLAME?"

Riddle-me-this was not the only game that *Tribune* copy editors began playing with the headlines, however. They were also fond of cryptograms. Too many readers, Denson seemed to feel, were scanning headlines and skipping stories. While he had a say in it, they would have to read the stories to find out what was going on. Some headlines became as obscure as the Tilden cipher dispatches. Such pretentious efforts as "PRESIDENT ON CENSORING: EXPLORATION & PROMISE" seemed to be promising an omniscience that the accompanying stories could not, unfortunately, live up to. Readers too soon realized that the body type made a liar out of the headlines. Many of the stories were merely warmed-over compilations of wire-service reports rewritten in the office with no more insight into background or true meaning of any event than was available, over the same wires, to any newspaper. And no amount of writing—to Denson's credit, he recognized and encouraged good writing—could gloss over the fact that the *Herald Tribune* was still being beaten on local stories. The paper's face might be changing, but one custom

remained intact. At 10:15 each weekday evening, when the *Times* came up, *Tribune* rewritemen were sent scurrying to their typewriters for "recoveries."

However effortless Denson's free-form kind of newspaper may have seemed to the reader, it did require the editor to spend hours puttering over makeup, contriving headlines, revising them and changing type size or play. Often he would still be at work after deadline, a situtation that sent the management analysts back to their slide rules. Late press runs, they warned Whitney, were costing him $85,000 a year, and reluctantly the publisher allowed *Herald Tribune* President Walter Thayer to issue Denson an ultimatum: either submit to the appointment of a "copy control editor" with the authority to put the paper in on time, or get out. Denson chose to get out, and the editorship of the *Tribune* devolved on a young man Denson himself had hired away from the Miami *Daily News*, James G. Bellows. Just after the change at the helm, in October, 1962, the paper's momentum was cruelly slowed by the first of the series of labor shutdowns that eventually convinced the publisher that there was no future for the *Herald Tribune*. The major editorial development of the Bellows regime was destined to be the "Sunday Punch," a highly promoted facelifting of the Sunday paper.

But whatever the *Herald Tribune*'s journalistic prospects may have been, the primary cause of its suspension remains the culmination of its lifelong Cain-Abel relationship with Horace Greeley's other child, Typographical Union Number Six—and the other nine newspaper unions that descended from it. After the 114-day shutdown of 1962–63, the paper shut down again in September, 1964, to honor its gentleman's agreement with the struck *Times*. Whitney kept faith with his fellow publishers for seven days and then, belatedly, he re-

opened the doors of the *Herald Tribune*. The step came too late to save the paper—merger talks were well under way.

On March 21, 1966, Whitney, William Randolph Hearst, Jr., and Roy Howard announced the formation of the World Journal Tribune Corporation, which, they hoped, would publish the *Herald Tribune* in the morning, a combined *World Journal* in the evening, and a doubly combined *World Journal Tribune* on Sundays. Immediately, difficulties sprang up—the principal one involving manning requirements of the unions and the question of layoffs. When negotiations dragged on without resolution, it became apparent that yet another strike was destined to accompany the formation of the merged enterprise on April 25.

When the writers and editors of the *Herald Tribune* set to work on the last paper on Saturday, April 23, there was little indication that there would, somehow, be a tomorrow. Still, as it had for a century and a quarter, the work of the paper went on. Stories were written, edited, and set into type, and papers came off the presses, to be hawked about the city just as in the days of Horace Greeley. Shortly before 10 P.M., Inky Blackman finished the news story that was to be the *Tribune*'s final word. True to *Tribune* tradition, it was well written. Fittingly, it was an obituary.

Mr. Shapiro worked on the Herald Tribune's *rewrite desk from 1962 to 1965. He is now on the staff of* The New Yorker.

The major source for the last century of the Tribune's *history is* The New York Tribune Since the Civil War, *by Harry Baehr, Jr. (Dodd, 1936). Other important sources include* Horace Greeley, Nineteenth Century Crusader, *by Glyndon G. Van Deusen (University of Pennsylvania Press, 1953); and* The Life of Whitelaw Reid, *by Royal Cortissoz (Scribner, 1921).*

John Hay Whitney

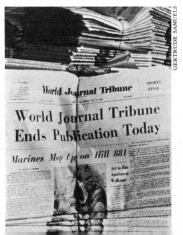